AN ORI
HOVE

CO N
US UIDE

NIKON

F70/D - N70/D

HOVE FOTO BOOKS

John Clements

Nikon F70 (International)
Nikon N70 (North America)

Nikon F70/N70

First English Edition February 1995

Published by Hove Foto Books Limited
Hotel de France, St Saviour's Road
St Helier, Jersey, Channel Islands, JE2 7LA
Tel: (01534) 614700 Fax: (01534) 887342

Typeset by Jersey Photographic Museum

Printed by
The Guernsey Press Co Ltd, Commercial Printing Division
Guernsey, Channel Islands

British Library Cataloguing-in-Publication Data
A catalogue record for this book is available from the British Library

Clements John - Nikon F70/N70

ISBN: 1-874031-70-3

Worldwide Distribution:

Newpro (UK) Ltd
Old Sawmills Road
Faringdon, Oxon.
SN7 7DS, England
Tel: (01367) 242411 Fax: (01367) 241124

Contents

Page No.

Introducing the F70/N70 6
Ergonomics, Build Quality and Control Layout 8
Getting Started - A Trip Around the Controls 11
Viewfinder Information 14
F70D/N70D Panoramic/Data Back Camera 19
The Body Control Points 32
Function Button 33
Set/Self-Timer Button 34
In/Out Buttons 35
Film Rewind Button 1 36
Ps (Vari-Program) Button 38
Autofocus Detection Area Button 38
On/Off Button 39
The Liquid Crystal Display 39
The Green Zone 40
Automatic Exposure Bracketing 40
Exposure Compensation with Daylight or Flash 40
Flash Mode 41
Metering Mode 41
Exposure Mode 41
Focus Mode Indication 42
Motor Driven Advance 42
Film Speed Setting 42
Shutter Speed & 'F' Stop Indications 43
Changing Lenses 43
The Rest of the Body 45
Automatic Exposure Lock Button 45
Loading the F70/N70 46
Creating Memorable Images 47
Light Measurement 47
3D Matrix Metering 48
Advanced 8-Segment Matrix Metering 51
Centre-Weighted Metering 54
Spot Metering 55
Exposure - Bringing The Image To Life 59
Manual Exposure Mode 60

Page No.

Bulb Exposures 61
Aperture-Priority Exposure Mode 62
Depth Of Field 62
Shutter-Priority 65
Auto-Multi Program 67
Flexible Program 68
Vari-Program (Ps) 69
Portrait Program 71
Hyperfocal Program 71
Landscape Program 72
Close-Up Program 72
Sports Program 73
Silhouette Program 73
Night Scene Program 74
Motion Effect Program 74
Exposure Compensation 75
Exposure Bracketing 76
Focusing - Seeing Is Believing 77
New Autofocus Module 77
Wide Area AF 78
Spot AF 80
Flash Photography 83
Auto Flash Control 84
TTL Flash Photography 85
18% Grey Reflective Shutter 87
The Built-In Speedlight 88
Special Flash Photography Techniques 89
Rear Curtain TTL Flash 90
Slow Synchronisation Flash 91
Standard TTL Flash Control 93
Balanced Fill Flash and Fill Flash 93
Synchronisation Speed 94
TTL Flash Compensation 95
TTL Flash Exposure Bracketing 96
Customising the F70/N70 - Choosing Accessories 101
SB26 Speedlight...124
Filters...125
LCD Panel/Viewfinder Indications 131

Nomenclature

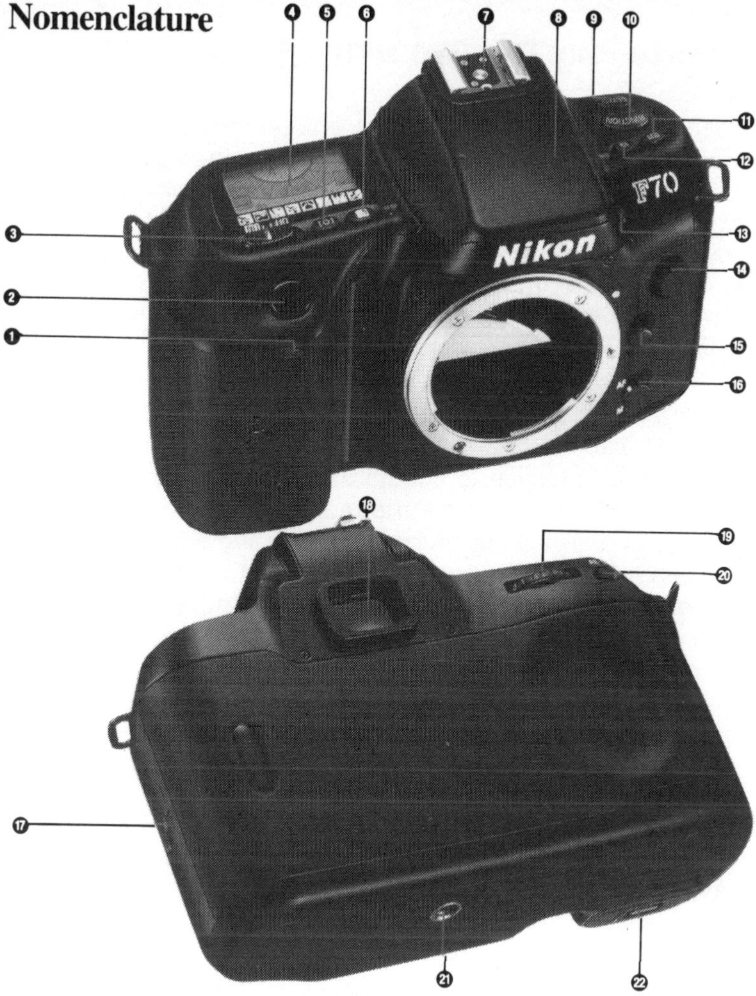

❶ Self-timer indicator LED
❷ Shutter release button
❸ Power switch
❹ LCD panel
❺ Focus area button
❻ Vari-Program (Ps)/film rewind button
❼ Accessory shoe
❽ Built-in Speedlight
❾ SET/⏲ button
❿ FUNCTION button
⓫ QR call (OUT) button
⓬ QR set (IN)/film rewind button
⓭ Flash lock-release button
⓮ Remote terminal
⓯ Lens release button
⓰ Focus mode selector
⓱ Camera back lock release
⓲ Viewfinder eyepiece
⓳ Command input control dial
⓴ AE-L (auto exposure lock) button
㉑ Tripod socket
㉒ Battery chamber cover lock release

Introducing The F70/N70

When Nikon launch a new camera, a great deal of interest is shown by both professional and enthusiast users. A company whose reputation was made by producing tough, reliable products, for the working pro, has in the last decade moved very much into the "new technology" arena, making equally reliable products with such advanced features as autofocus and clever metering systems for the non professional.

With the introduction of the F70/N70 and F70D/N70D (quartz data back fitted, with a panoramic format option), Nikon has confirmed its intention to update the autofocus cameras of the early 1990's to more modern cameras that have advanced on a number of fronts. While the F70/N70 and F70D/N70D cameras are primarily offered to the amateur photographer who possesses an advanced level of knowledge in both camera operation and the techniques of photography, they are also blessed with the point and shoot needs of the novice. It will also find its way into professional hands like many Nikon cameras do as a spare body, being lighter and cheaper to purchase than the next camera in the line, the F90/N90. This is particularly the case if Nikon's motorised AFI lenses are used - the F70/N70 is fully compatible with them and it is no accident that many of the F70/N70 features are based on the award winning F90/N90 series.

However, its long list of specification means that there is often some confusion about how to operate specific features and the benefits they may, or may not, offer. Sadly due to cost and space limitations, some of the publications that accompany cameras like this are a little thin on supporting information. That is why I am pleased to offer this book. I have used the F70/N70 extensively and have learned much about it that does not originate from the instruction manuals.

We start by taking an informative look at the layout of body controls, moving on to talk about the Liquid Crystal Display panels and commenting on the newly designed focusing screen that many reviews have all but ignored. As you progress through this book discover as I have the benefits and limitations of the F70/N70. I hope you enjoy the explanation as to "how and why" specific features such as autofocus (AF) and 3D Matrix metering operate. In all chapters I have taken the theory of what the camera sets out to do and set it against the needs of real photography.

For those of us who earn our living from the medium, understanding the "tools of the trade" is paramount if we are to produce the quality of results desired, without continuous and time consuming references to instruction manuals. For those who enjoy photography as a hobby it seems to me a shame that some possibilities are often missed through a lack of understanding of the cameras owned. Whatever your needs - good photography!

John

December 1994

CREDITS

The publishers would like to thank Nikon UK, in Singapore, the Nikon Distributors, our model Alice (who works in the Nikon Service Department) and Dennis Pang from Readers Choice for their assistance.
Colour photos taken in Singapore by Hove Foto Books Staff.

Chapter One
Ergonomics, Build Quality And Control Layout

Ergonomics - is the term given to the art of design that make products suited to the human form.

Some cameras seem to fit into our hands far more comfortably than others with the controls in the right place for easy use. Ultimately, attempting to design a camera where the ergonomics are pleasing to all is probably impossible as we are all of different shapes, sizes and tastes. Even so, do you find the F70/N70 comfortable to hold? When I first picked one up, it felt comfortable with the camera to my eye - not because of the light weight, but because there is a large grip where our right hand rests. The camera to our eye is more important in comfort terms than in our hands as this is the position of the camera when most pictures are taken. As most are handheld, a comfortable camera and lens combination makes for more stable pictures than an uncomfortable one.

We will comment on the positioning and feel of the camera controls a little later, but what about the weight of the camera? The F70/N70 is a major departure from many previous Nikon cameras in that it makes use of less metal in its construction than its forebears, with many plastic components being preferred. A hybrid design has been used for the lens mount, mirror box and shutter mechanisms. The weight of the body alone is only 585 grams for the F70/N70 body and 600 grams for the F70D/N70D. This is without batteries.

Did You Know? - The term "mirror box" refers to a part of the camera in which all of the components for controlling the mirror are housed.

Do not be put off by the light weight, or my comments regarding the use of plastics. The plastics used have been specially selected to meet Nikon's requirements and some important parts such as the lens mount and film guide rails inside the camera back are still made from the most stable, time proven material - metal. It is interesting that some companies use plastic guide rails in cameras that will not get heavy daily use. This is something Nikon have so far not used. Plastic can warp more easily than metal in hot conditions and can lead to the distance from the lens to the film not being a constant. This in turn, particularly with long lenses and shallow depth of field, may lead to a slightly out of focus image.

The "F" mount is still employed on the front of the camera and will accept more lenses from both the autofocus (AF) and manual focus (MF) lens line up than other makes of camera.

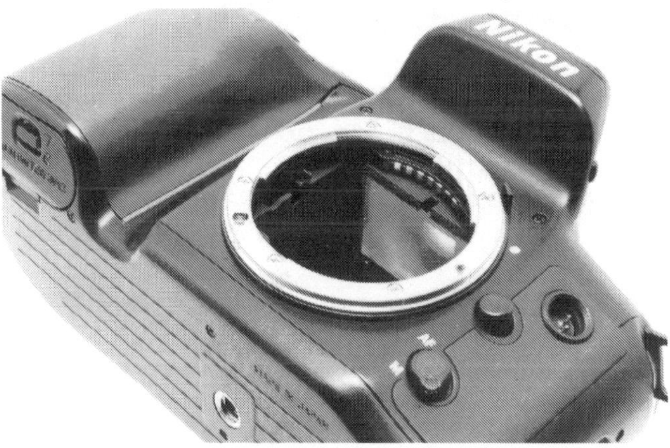

This too remains metal and is held securely against the body by five screws - a proven design. More on lenses in Chapter 6 - Customising the F70/N70.

So, let us get started in using the camera. If you are already familiar with the F70/N70 you may wish to move onto the next chapter 'Creating Memorable Images'.

Powering an F70/N70

Another major departure from the traditional Nikon design concept has been with the choice of the power source. In most recent Nikon cameras four AA size alkaline manganese batteries have been used. This has proved popular with professionals and amateurs alike as they are easy to come by, relatively cheap, and if the camera batteries fail there are often replacements readily available in other equipment like flash units and walkmans etc.. For those who work in cold conditions - around zero degrees or lower - many cameras accept AA size Nickel Cadmium cells and often an external anti-cold battery pack to keep the cells warm against the body, with a lead running into the camera's battery chamber.

While I still feel strongly that the AA size option should be available on a camera, I can see that the choice of two lithium CR123A cells was made on probably three counts. First the lithium cells do give 3 volts output each, so the 6 volts that most cameras operate on are reached, leading to the second point that the two lithium cells take up less space for the same output as four AA alternatives. The final benefit is that Lithium cells are less likely to leak than alkaline manganese.

On the base of the camera (to the right side) is a small hinged door marked with a symbol like a character from the "Packman" computer game. Above it is a triangle sign pointing towards it. This door does not remove completely. Just pull on the small plastic tab to allow access to the battery chamber which is the supposed indication of the "Packman" symbol. Inside the chamber is a diagram to indicate the way to fit the batteries with the plus and minus terminals in the correct direction. On the underside of the door is again an indication of battery positioning. The door can then be pushed closed until it clicks. When we replace batteries it is a good idea to replace both of them at the same time - yes, I do realise the cost!

When we switch the F70/N70 'on' a battery symbol appears on the top right side of the Liquid Crystal Display (L.C.D.). Strangely this is in the shape of an AA cell! If the batteries are giving their full output the cell should be shaded in with just one small break in the shading about 2/3rds along the symbol.

As the cells near exhaustion the shading will start to progressively disappear. There is no need to change batteries however until the whole battery symbol blinks. There is no external anti-cold battery pack for the F70/N70 as lithium batteries work in sub-zero temperatures. One other indication of the battery condition is the length of time that the viewfinder and some of the top-plate displays last. When the output is normal the readout should stay on for about 8 seconds.

In the instruction manual, Nikon state that fresh batteries should give us 115 rolls of 36 exposure film if we don't use flash, and 25 if we use the built-in flash unit for half of the shots. This translates into 172.5 rolls of 24 exposure film without flash and 37.5 with flash used half of the time. Before we take things out of perspective however, this is based on one lens - 28mm-70mm f3.5/4.5 when focused from infinity (∞) to its closest distance and back again. Continuous Servo AF and continuous high speed film advance (CH) also operate, while a shutter speed of at least a 1/125th of a second is used and all this is at around 20° centigrade. One more thing - the batteries are also very fresh. While we all need a guide, do bear in mind that when we "play" with the camera to get used to it, we are using up power. Another type of lens or operating feature will also act differently on the rate of exhaustion.

Getting Started - A Trip Around The Controls

The ON/OFF control is situated on the camera's top-plate above the L.C.D. panel. The camera can only be set to either ON or OFF. A secure click is heard when we switch from one to the other. I found that the resistance is just right to stop the camera being turned ON or OFF accidentally. It is sloped to enable the pad on our finger to fall into it - a nice ergonomic touch! A white line in the middle of the switch rests against either the word OFF or ON below the switch depending upon the setting.

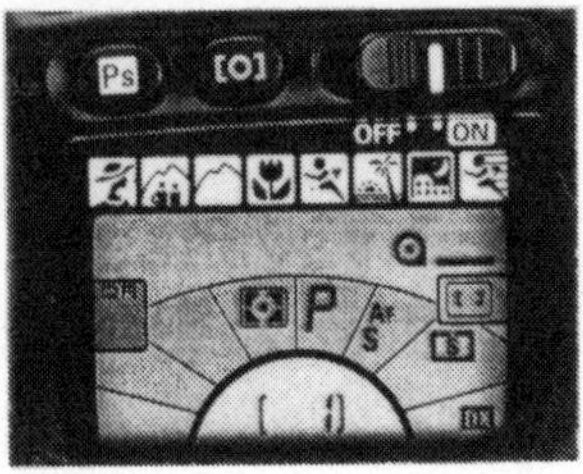

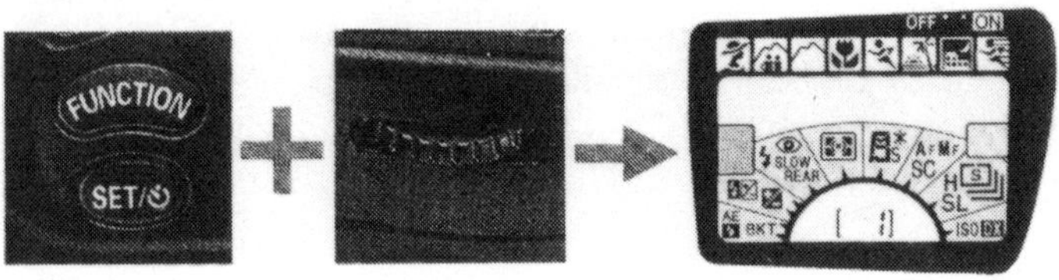

The F70/N70, like all modern Nikons (except the F4 series), uses a Command Input Dial as its main control centre. This is the dial that pokes out of the rear of the top-plate below the L.C.D. panel.

Very few features of the camera are set without this dial being rotated. What I recommend, so that we can start from the same starting point, is that you have the camera set to those features that are the standard settings with which it left the factory. The following steps will set the camera in such a way, no matter what the camera was previously set to.

A. With the camera ON and an AF Nikkor lens attached and set to the "F" stop number marked in orange, look at the left topside of the camera. There is a button marked 'OUT' in yellow. Press and hold down on this button.

B. Rotate the Command Input Dial anti-clockwise. On the top-plate L.C.D. there is a portion marked in yellow in the shape of a small square. Inside are the letters QR which stand for Quick Recall. Turn the Command Input Dial until the number 0 appears. Then release pressure from the Command Input Dial and the OUT button. We have now set the camera to its most automated features of:-

- Single frame film advance speed each time we release the shutter once.
- Wide Area autofocus.
- Automatic Auto-Multi pattern.
- Matrix metering.

Did You Know? - The size of the opening in a lens is called the "F" stop. For any Programmed or Shutter-Priority exposure modes the largest number, marked in orange, must be selected or else the camera will not fire. The letters FEE are displayed on the L.C.D. panels as a warning if not set and the F70/N70 refuses to fire.

With the shutter release button touched gently, various numerals and figures will appear on both the camera's top-plate and inside the viewfinder. If we took a photograph now the camera would set all controls, using Auto-Multi Program exposure control and 3D Matrix metering. All we have to do is decide to use autofocus or manual focus - so let's start with that control.

AF/MF Switch - This control is situated on the camera's front. Turn the camera so you are looking directly at the front. In the bottom right corner there is a switch. Marked on it is a white spot. With a decisive movement we can set the switch to the A for autofocus or M for manual focus. Be careful, however, as it is possible to set the spot to an intermediate point. For now, move the control to the A position for autofocus.

So to recap. For the easiest way to use an F70/N70, select the number 0 in the small yellow square on the top-plate, turn the "F" stop number to the orange setting and move the focus control to either M or A as desired.

Viewfinder Information

Now let us look into the viewfinder. If you are familiar with cameras from previous decades, you will straight away appreciate the bright viewfinder image. This is due to the new type of Nikon screen called a BriteView II. As each generation of camera passes so it seems that a new screen design is introduced as well. The effects of the BriteView screen II are subtle compared to the original BriteView screen still employed in other Nikon AF S.L.R. cameras.

As with all things there are both benefits and drawbacks. In making focusing screens brighter all manufacturers have had to make do with screens that in the right circumstances exhibit annoying habits. Specifically, the use of long focal lengths and teleconverters can introduce an effect of moire patterning. What we see is a rainbow-like break up of colours on the focusing screen. They would not show on the final image as this is just an effect seen in the viewfinder, but it can still be annoying. In reality however few people experience the problem as it is rare for the exact combinations to occur. For those that often do have problems professional cameras such as the F4 with special, but less, bright screens can be used.

Another effect that the new screen overcomes is something to which few people have given a thought. When we look at a part of a focusing screen that covers an out-of-focus point, the screen displays this part of an image in a different way to that seen with the naked eye. The new screen is claimed to be more natural in this respect. For most of us however our prime concern is that the image we see on the focusing screen is bright and uncluttered. In this respect the new screen is definitely a winner! There has also been a claimed increase in the "bite" to the image seen when we manually focus and reach the correct point. This has been a criticism of other BriteView screens in the past that don't give an image that jumps into focus which earlier non BriteView screens do, such as those found in the F3 and FM2 cameras.

On the focusing screen are a small number of etched markings. These indicate the major metering area of the Centre-Weighted metering option (large circle), the area of Spot metering (small circle), and the autofocus detection areas - Wide AF (oblong jaws) and Spot AF once again the small circle.

Sadly the screen fitted cannot be removed or replaced by a grid screen or other alternatives. As this camera is meant to attract some of the F801s/N8008s users, this is an omission that I think is dubious. However the majority of people using a F70/N70 will do so quite happily and not give screen interchangeability a second thought. If the screen does become damaged the whole camera must be returned to a Nikon service facility.

There are a few points worth reminding people about. The first is that when we look through the viewfinder of an F70/N70, we see around 92% of the image that will be recorded on film. This equates nicely to the image seen, important for transparencies put into mounts. For those who prefer colour negative film it is not that far away from showing the area in our final pictures as most processing machines crop a small portion as well.

As for viewfinder accessories it is worth considering the following:-

The F70/N70 comes with an eyepiece cover called a DK5. This is meant to cover the eyepiece when we are taking pictures but not looking through the camera at the same time. This stops light entering the viewfinder and misleading the metering cells that are housed inside the prism of the camera. The only light we want them to register is that which comes through a lens from our subject. I would also recommend attaching a very nice rubber eye cup called a DK9. This creates a light trap to stop light entering the viewfinder and reducing the crispness or, as we call it, the contrast of the image. It also helps those who wear glasses from scratching them on the viewfinder eyepiece. The final accessory is a necessity for some - diopter correction lenses. The F70/N70 takes the same clip-on diopters as the F50/N50, F601/N6006 and F401/N5005 series of cameras.

Below the focusing screen is an L.C.D. panel that duplicates the most relevant information shown on the top-plate L.C.D.. Contrary to what may at first seem logical, there is not much benefit in crowding the viewfinder display with every piece of information. The reason is twofold. First, it would take too long to take in and digest and second, it often becomes redundant in the heat of the moment for those who are photographing a moving subject or one needing a constant stream of chatter on our part. Quite rightly we tend to concentrate on the image on the focusing screen and our comments, more than assessing a crowded L.C.D. panel. The F70/N70 has a display that is just about practical, although I have heard some people say it is too cluttered. In future cameras we will be able to decide what information is displayed and what is not. For now however let's concentrate on our F70/N70.

Seeing Is Believing

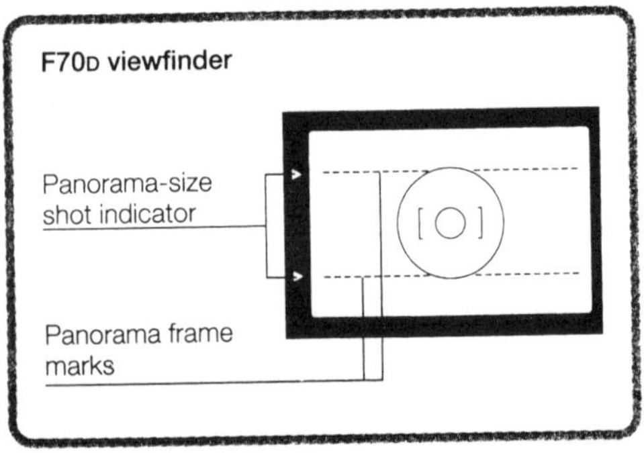

Nikon believe that most people will use the F70/N70 set to one of its autofocus modes. There are two types as we shall see later. Each has a symbol of recognition and this is the first symbol shown on the left of the viewfinder display. For Wide AF two oblong jaws are displayed inside an outer box. Spot AF is indicated by just that - a spot inside a box. If we are using manual focus (MF) then the last AF symbol that was in use is maintained. This is I think a mistake, as no symbol indicates when we have the camera set to MF.

The next symbol indicates the focus condition on the part of the image that the AF marker covers. A black spot is shown as a steady symbol if the electronics and related systems believe the image to be at its sharpest. If we are in manual focus the same spot is shown when we reach the focus point, but in addition a triangle is displayed indicating the direction in which we should turn the focusing ring until the spot appears by itself. When the two triangles are side by side and steady, a feature called Focus Tracking is active. The same triangles appear together but pulsate if the camera cannot find focus in AF or confirm it in MF.

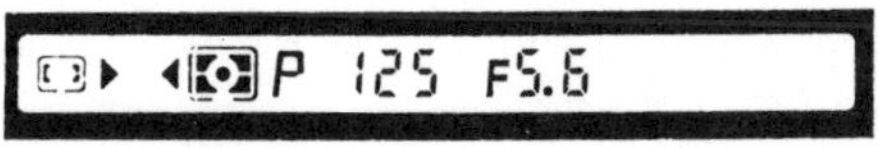

3D Matrix, Advanced 8-Segment Matrix, Centre-Weighted and Spot metering have their appropriate symbol shown to the right of the focus indication. When either of the two Matrix modes are operative the same symbol is used. A circle with two outer lines specify that Centre-Weighted operation is in use, while (no prizes for guessing) Spot metering will be represented by a spot.

The first letter of an exposure mode is used as the symbol to show our selection. This will mean that the following are shown when different modes are used:-

Program = P
Flexible Program = Ps
Shutter-Priority = S
Aperture-Priority = A
Manual = M

The approximated shutter speed the F70/N70 recommends is next to the centre of the display if we are using any Programmed mode or Aperture-Priority. The exact shutter speed set will be displayed if we are utilising Manual or Shutter-Priority. The F70/N70 and the F90/N90 cameras are the only Nikon S.L.R.s to display the shutter speed indication in 1/3rd E.V. steps. Occasionally the shutter speed may blink as an indication of potential camera shake.

Next to the shutter speed is the "F" stop number. This is an approximation if we are working in Programmed or Shutter-Priority, while Manual or Aperture-Priority are shown in exact amounts.

There will sometimes be a small bar graph display appearing to the right of the "F" stop value. A number of vertical lines appear under a scale that has a '+' at one end, a '0' in the middle and a '-' at the other end. It is called an Electronic Analog display.

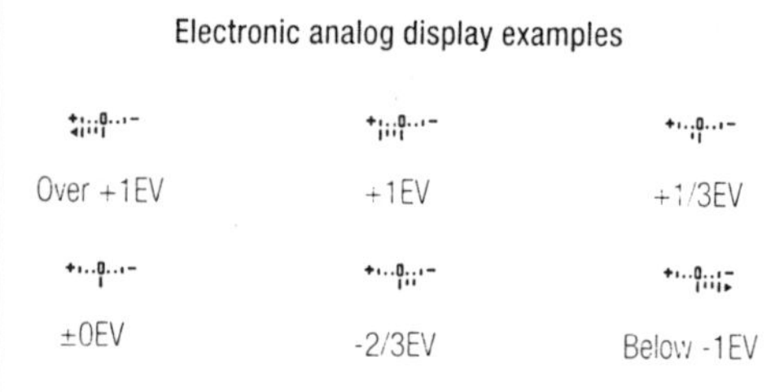

The electronic analog display blinks when the shutter speed/ aperture set on the camera is beyond the metering range of the F70/N70.

Two other symbols will occasionally appear depending upon whether we have selected the appropriate feature. Next, on the right of the Electric Analog, is a lightning bolt symbol. This will only show when we have compensated, or in other words adjusted, the output of the built-in flash unit or one that is fully compatible with the F70/N70.

Finally, on the right of the display panel we might see a +/- symbol. This appears when, and only when, we have adjusted one of the camera's automatic exposure modes -

Programmed, Flexible Program, Aperture-Priority or Shutter-Priority.

Other Points To Mention

The whole of the L.C.D. panel is automatically illuminated by the camera in low light. We should therefore not have to worry about a dark dingy display. The symbols will not all be on display together, thereby avoiding the problem I mentioned earlier. When you look through the viewfinder you see a good level of image contrast which is helped by proper matte black painting of the interior of the viewfinder.

One area of photographic technique that scares many people is flash photography.

This can range from the question of - "When do I need to use flash?" To - "How much flash do I need?" On the first point - when to use flash, the F70/N70 recommends its use to us. Along the left side (vertical) of the viewfinder is displayed a yellow lightning bolt which appears whenever the camera feels that flash illumination is beneficial. When a flash unit has charged, ready for use, a red lightning bolt above it is displayed and the yellow one goes out.

The display, like the top-plate L.C.D. lasts for eight seconds if we lightly touch the shutter release but take no pictures. If we do take a picture, the display goes off 2 seconds after the shot if we remove finger pressure from the release.

F70D/N70D Panoramic/Data Back Camera

If you own one of the F70D/N70D cameras one of its features is that of Panoramic format. This seems to have become very popular in Japan where most cameras are now made with it as a standard feature. In the rest of the world this has yet to catch on.

Did You Know? - Technically the term "Panoramic" is incorrect as the characteristic of such a format is to have an unusually long width for capturing panoramas. In 35mm cameras, however, the width of the image area is the same as the normal 35mm format, but parts from the top and bottom of the format are lost at the exposure stage. This is achieved by two internal baffles masking these areas from an exposure.

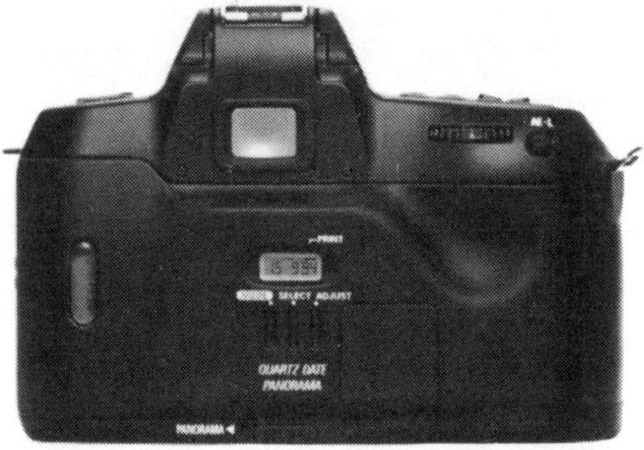

F70D/N70D with Date/Time imprinting and Panorama functions

If we use the panoramic feature there are, supplied with the F70/N70 instruction books, some stickers. Some say Panorama, others Normal and others Panorama mixed, while a third type states - Develop Only. The appropriate sticker should be attached onto the film cassette after exposure so our lab can make the adjustments to the print size if we have been using colour or black and white negative film. If we use transparency, the normal image area is shown inside the slide mount but with the top and bottom sections blacked out. Processing and printing labs should make prints on a slightly longer piece of paper than normal to give it the appearance of a panoramic image. Be careful though as panoramic may cost more at some labs. To guide us when we use this feature on the F70D/N70D are two dotted lines that show in the viewfinder when we use the panoramic feature. The insides of these indicate the area of our image. Above and

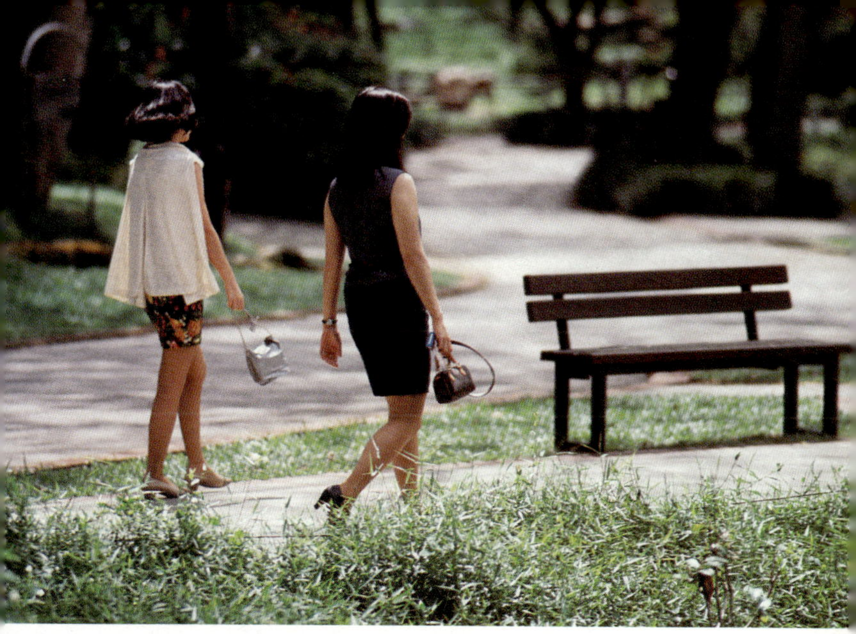

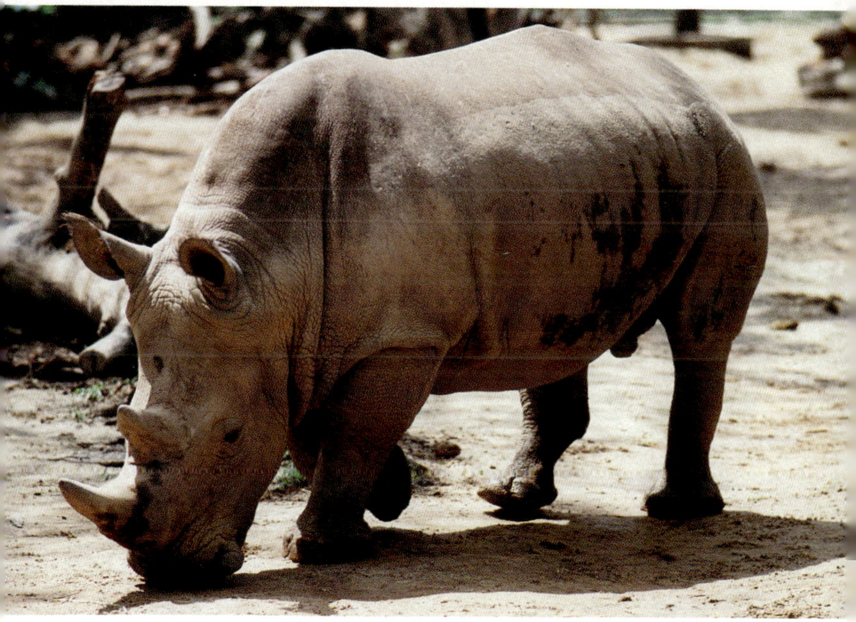

A day out at the zoo, with your Nikon F70/N70.
Do not forget a Tele lens, 180 or 70-210 zoom.

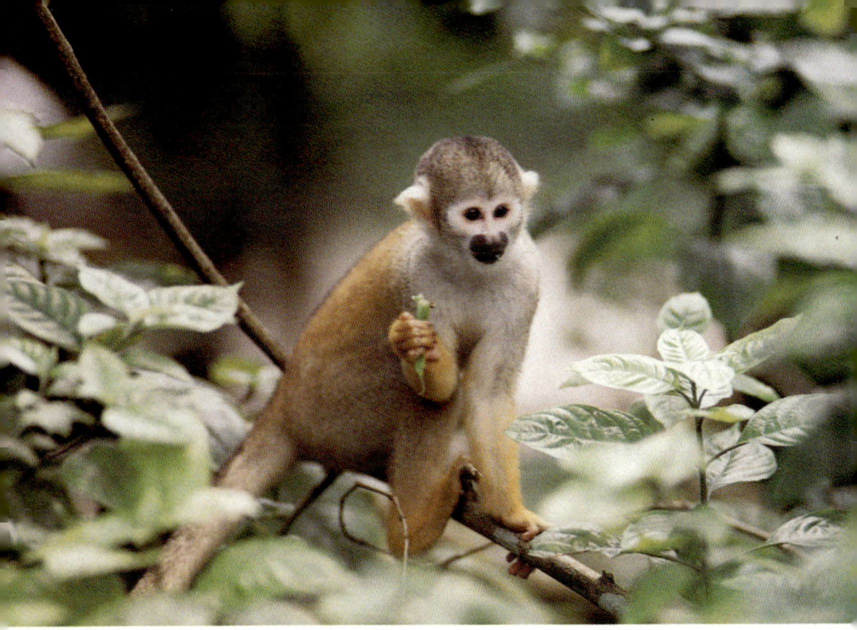

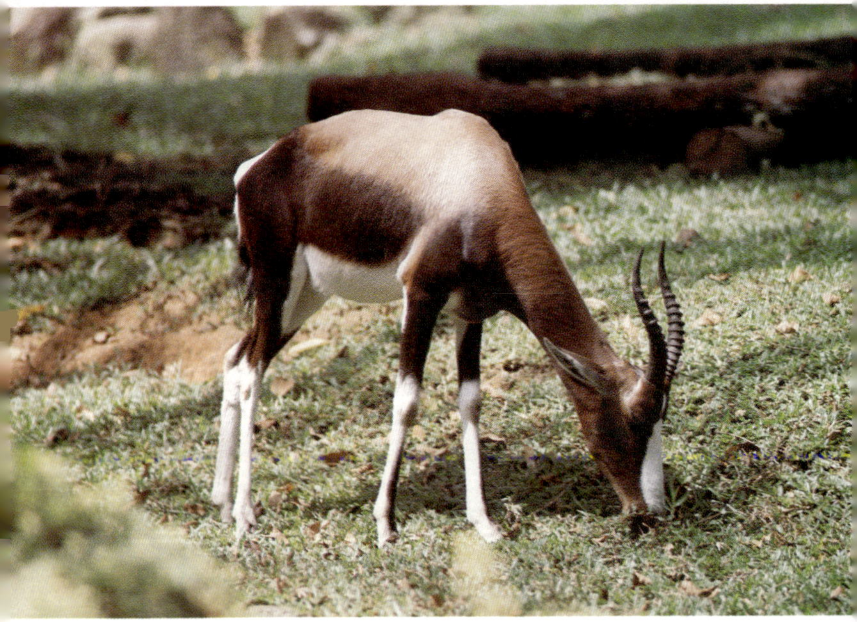

f2.8 on aperture priority auto, lens,
Nikon 180mm f2.8 A/F IFED + CL38 Hood

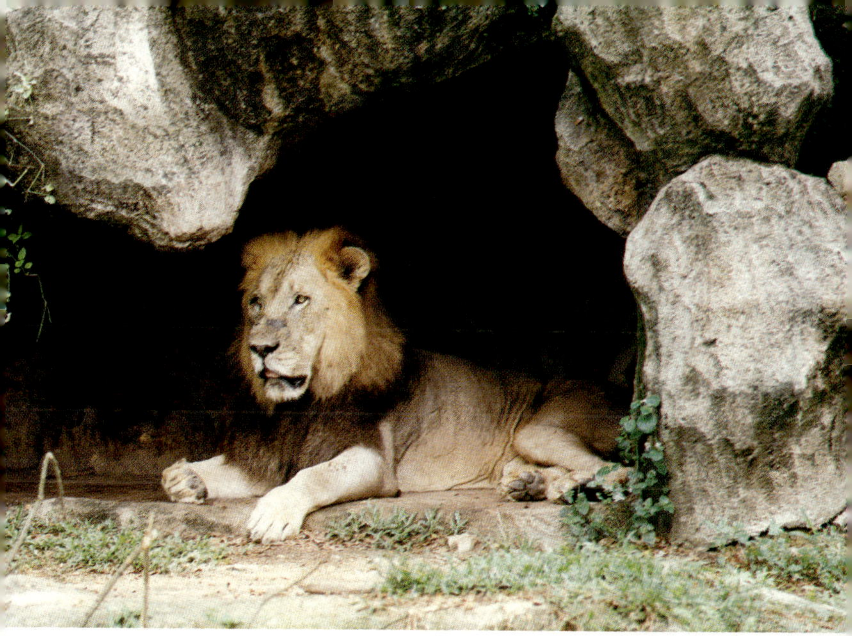

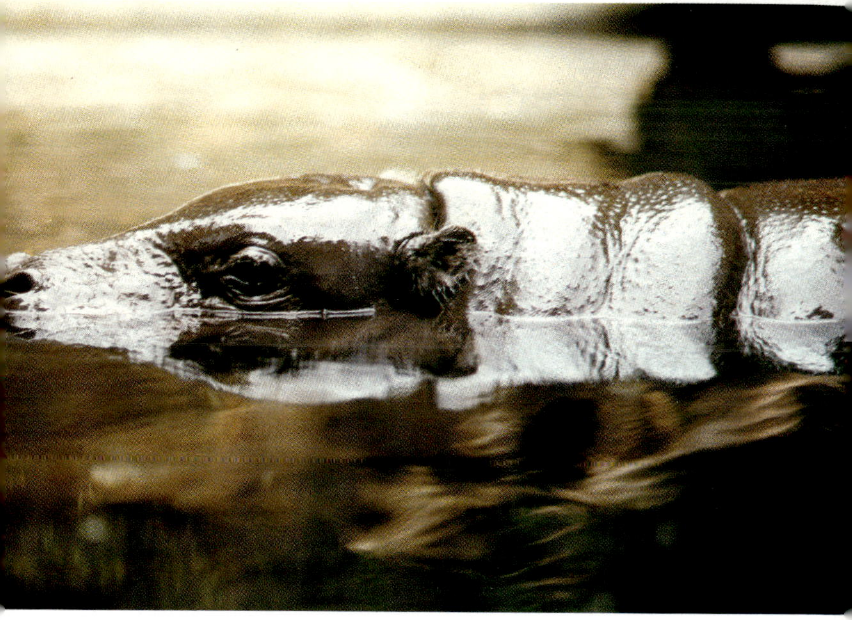

A Tele lens is a must, do not lean over protective fences or push camera through bars.

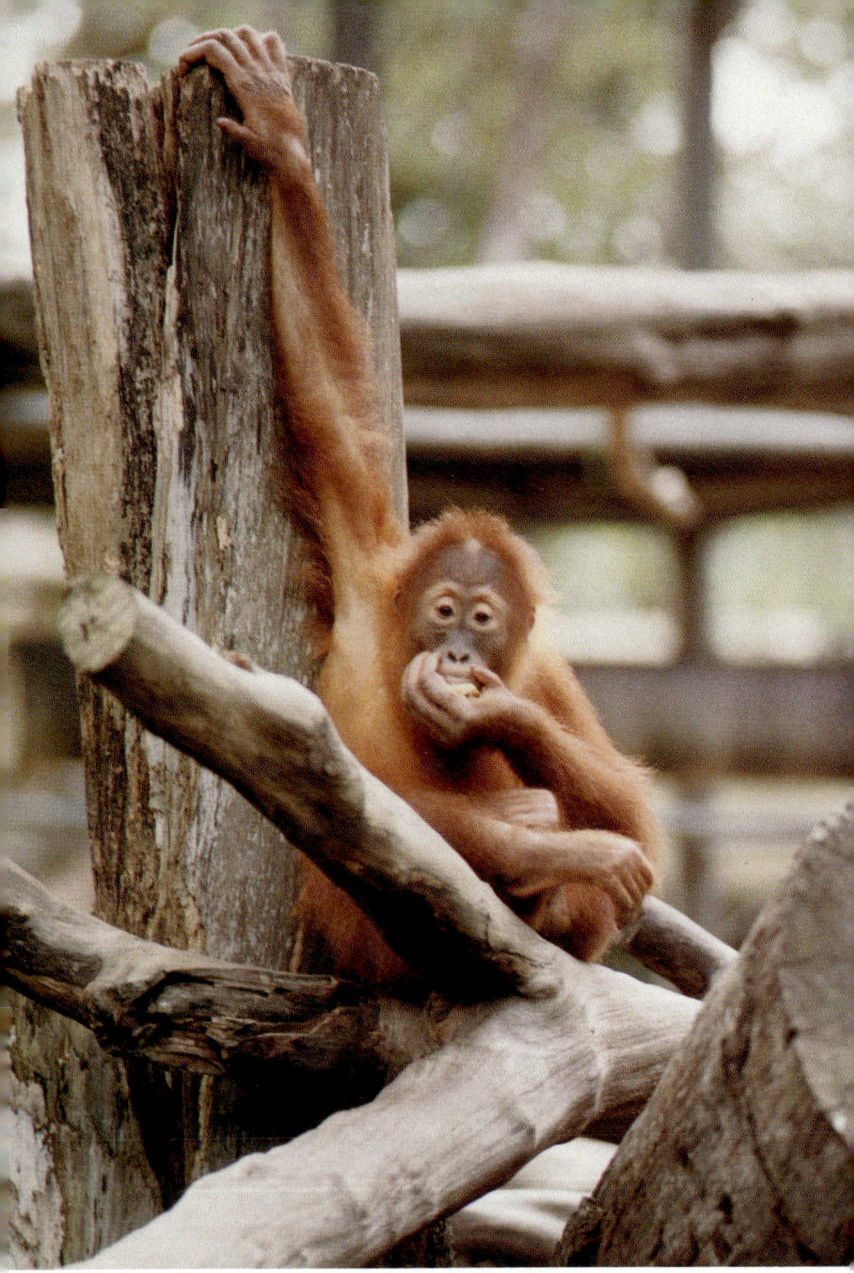

A 70-210 zoom lens, or a better option would be the 75-300 zoom lens for this shot.

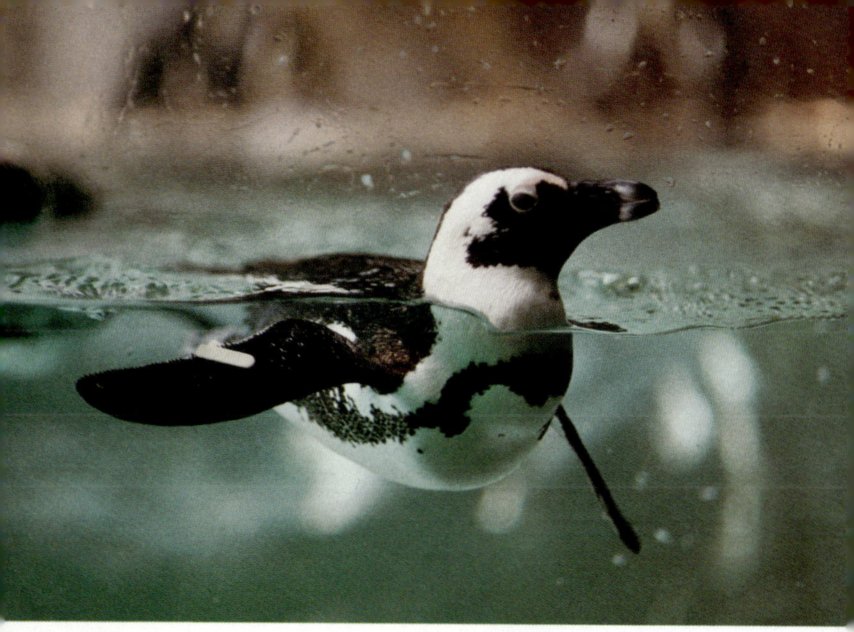

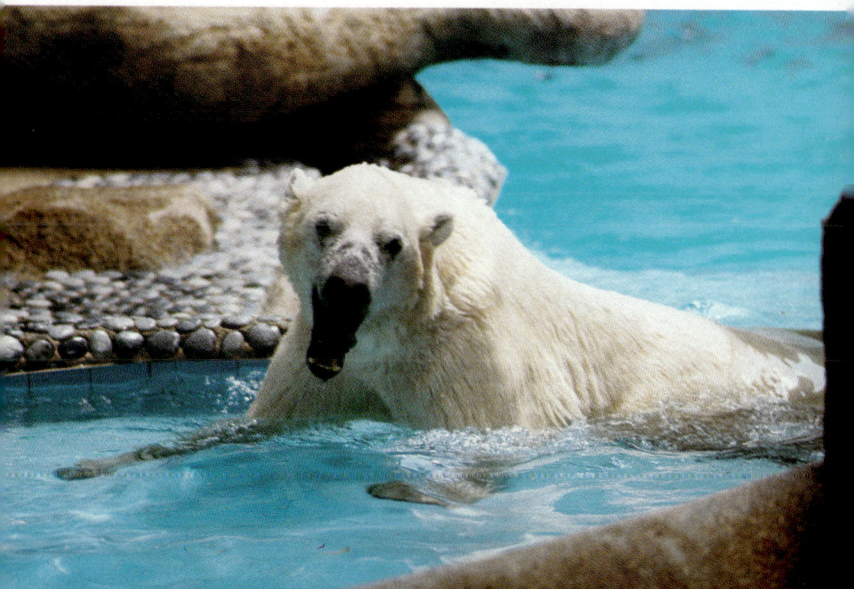

35-70 f2.8 zoom lens was used for these shots.
A fast lens helped with low light levels.

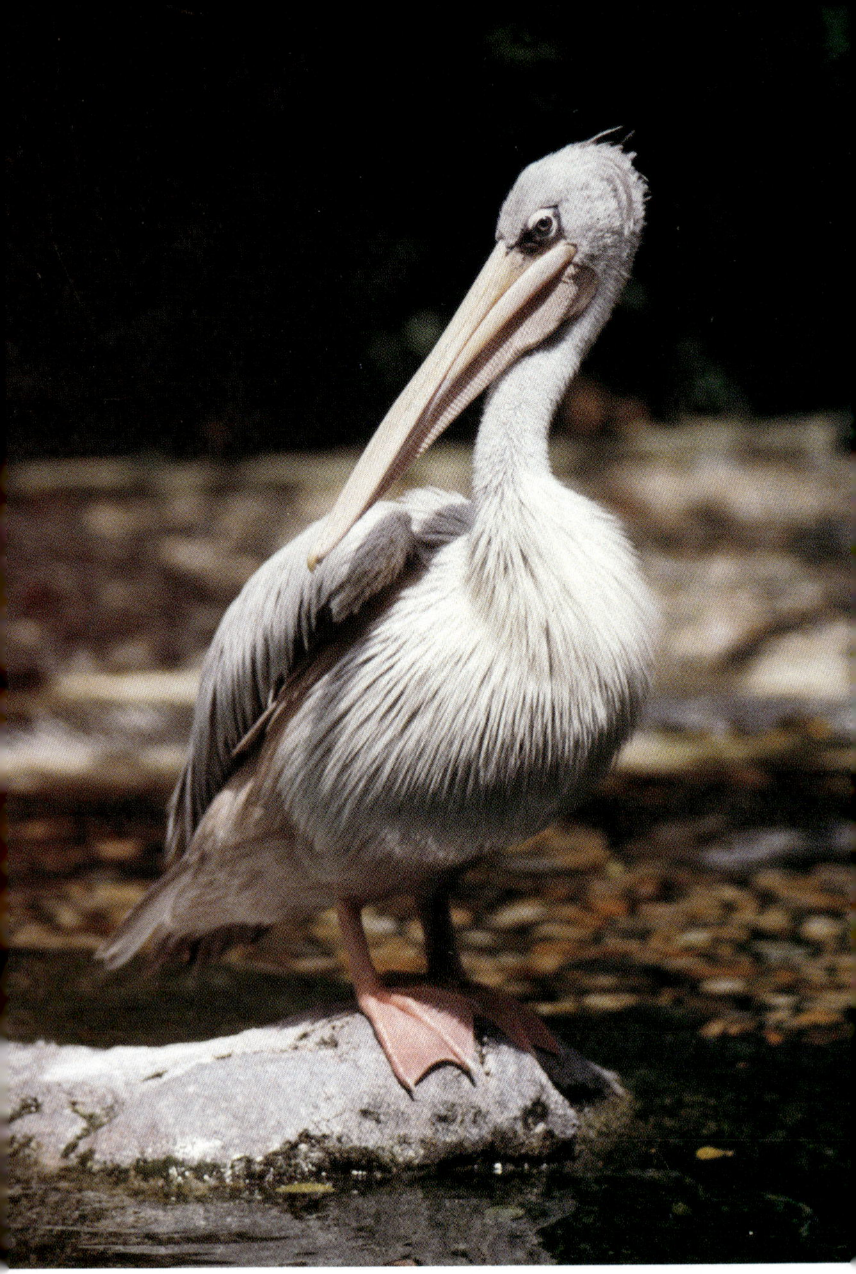

A polarising filter has helped to darken the background. With A/F cameras you must use a circular polariser.

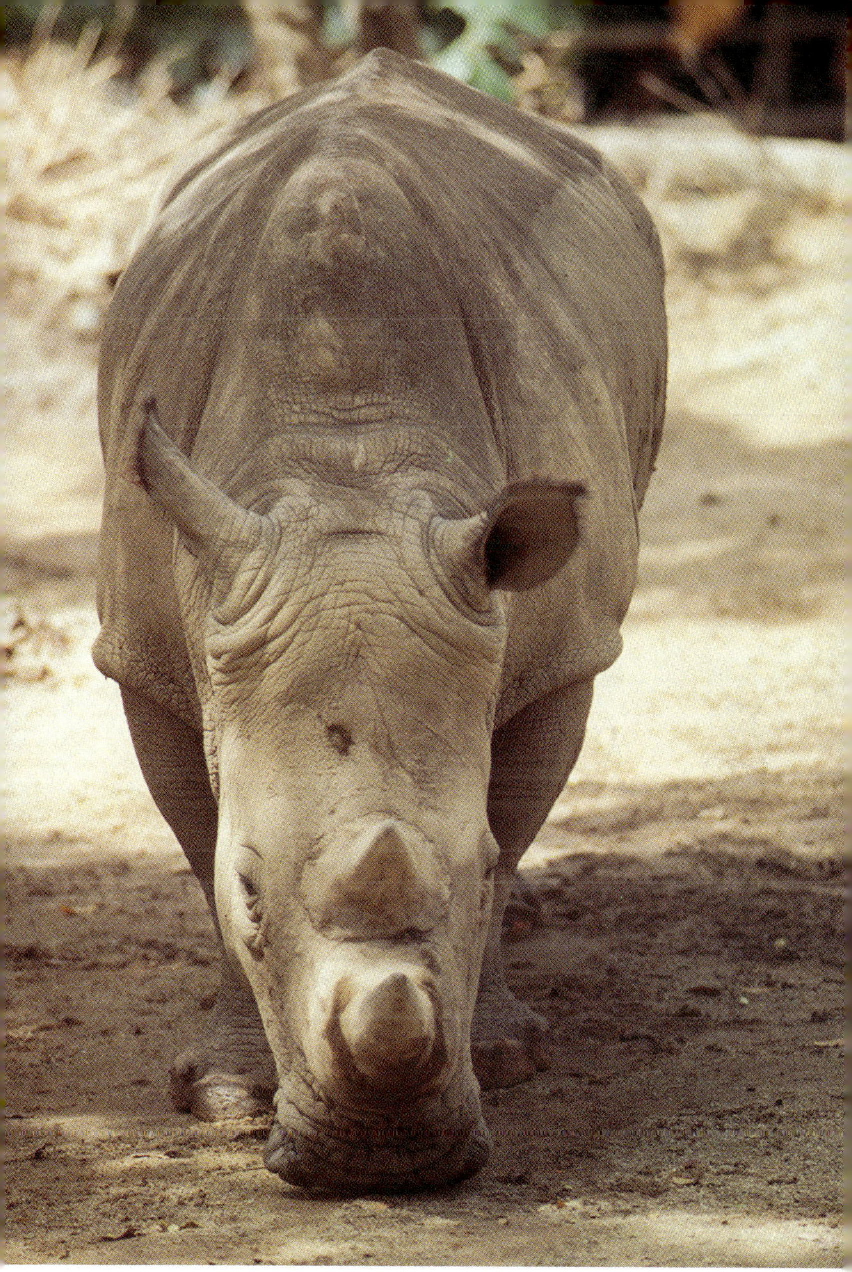

Programmed auto exposure control will allow you to take a similar shot and a quick get-away.

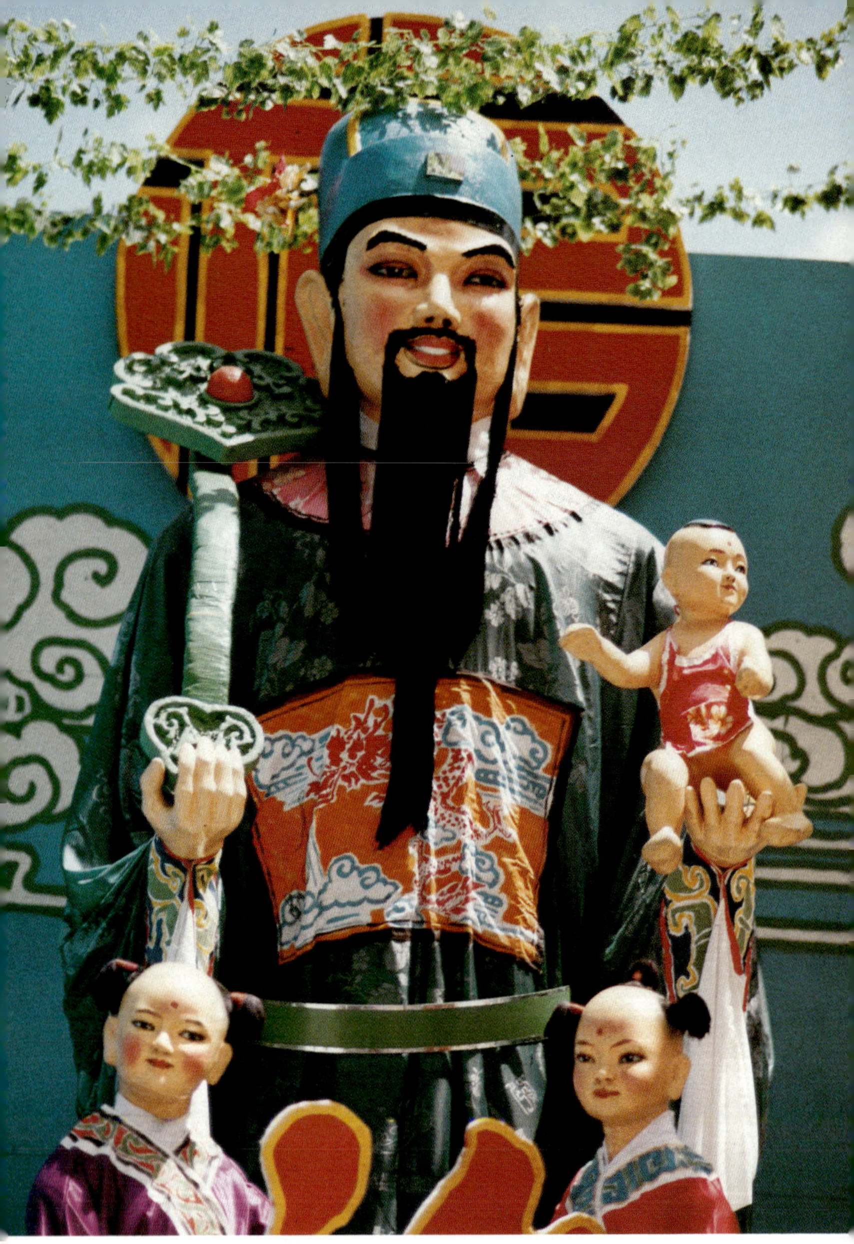

Theme parks provide many photographic opportunities.
Don't forget to use the cameras built in flash
to remove unwanted shadows.

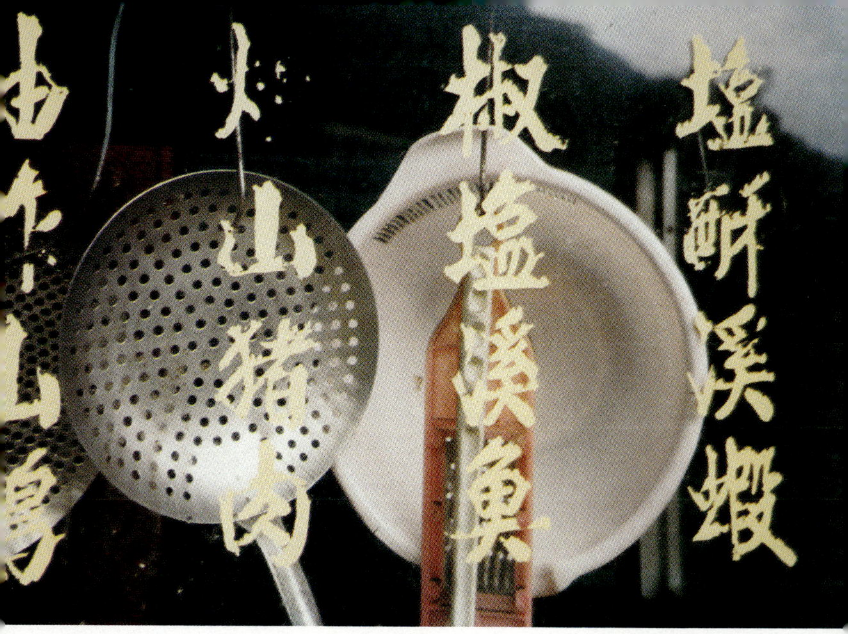

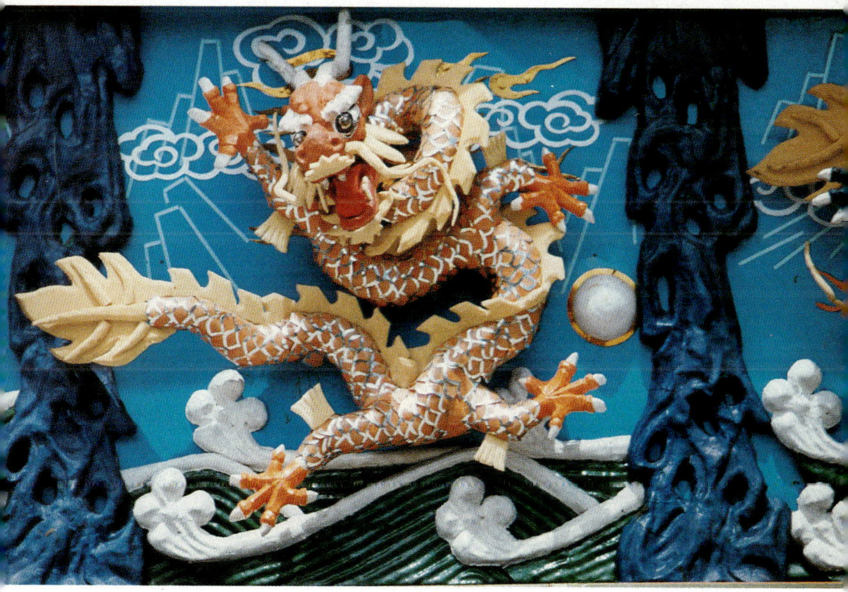

The days menu with background of kitchen utensils makes a different shot. Above Chinese dragon heralds another New Year.

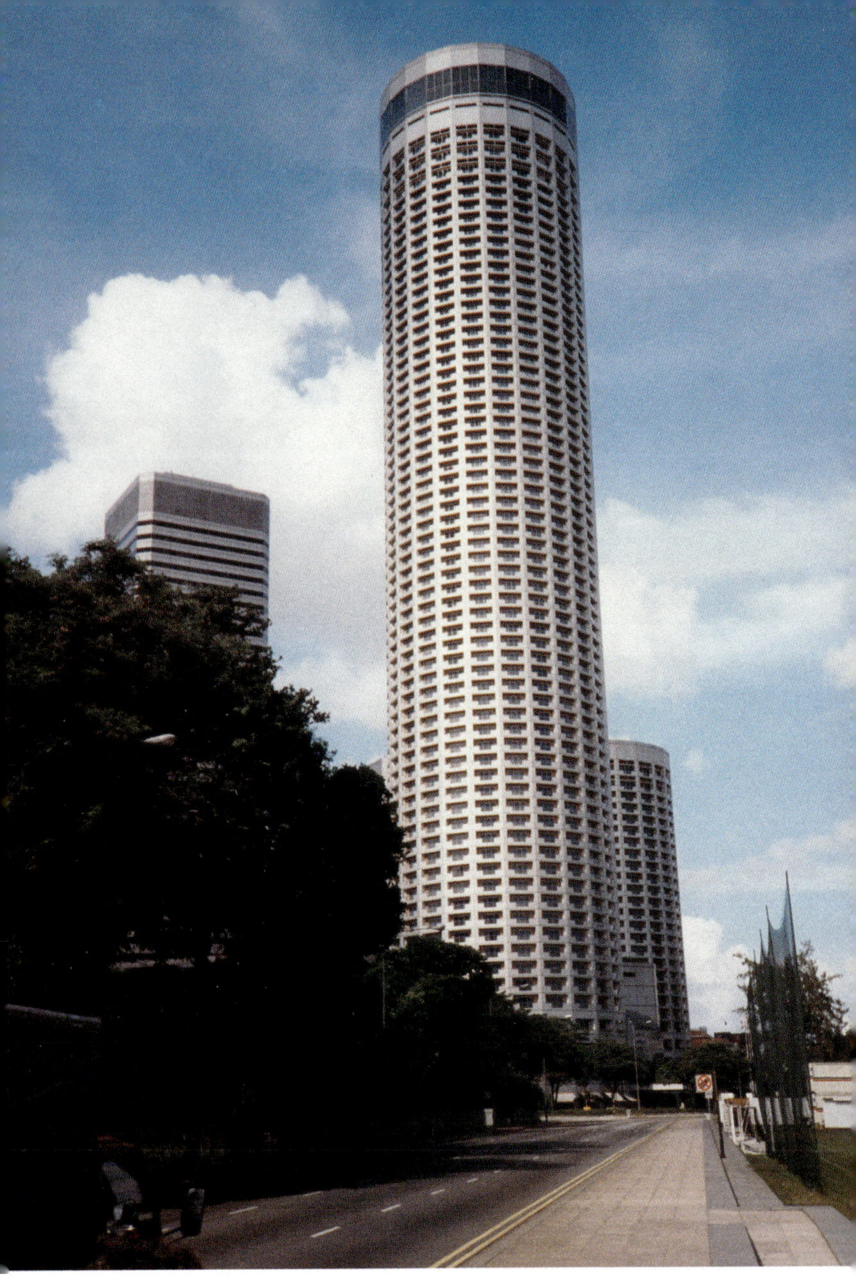

The Singapore Westin Hotel, the tallest hotel in the world, 20-35 f2.8 zoom lens

below the two lightning bolt symbols, that glow when flash use is recommended or when the flash is charged, are two triangles parallel with the panoramic lines. They glow red when this format is in operation.

On the back of the F70D/N70D there is a switch that moves from left to right. One position (with letter P showing) is the panoramic format setting. Two jaws have masked off part of the image area at this time. Nikon do not recommended that shutter speeds below 1/15th of a second are used as they claim that sunlight entering the lens may damage the shutter curtains that make up the mask. I find this a little bit dubious but safety first is recommended.

Also on the back of the F70D/N70D is a databack that will, if we wish, print on our picture -

Year/Month/Day
Day/Hour/Minute
Month/Day/Year
Day/Month/Year

The imprint can be turned off when no readout is shown on the back's L.C.D..

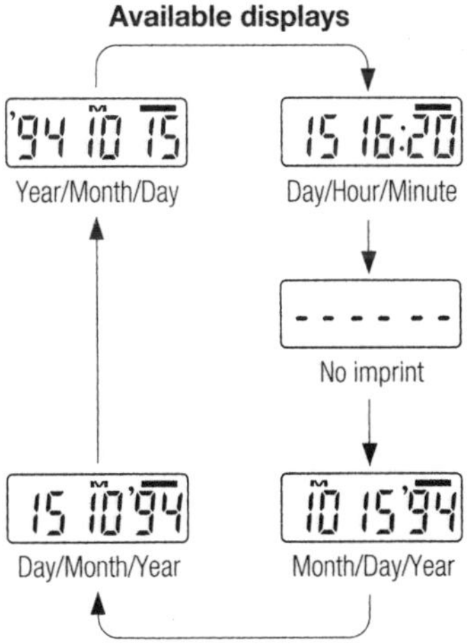

The imprint appears in the bottom right of both the panoramic and normal format depending upon whichever one has been set.

Unfortunately the F70D/N70D was not on the market when I wrote this book so I apologise for not being able to comment on it a little further. To the best of my knowledge it is identical in all other ways to the F70/N70.

Q. The image I see on the focusing screen is not sharp, why?

A. Providing we or the camera have focussed correctly, it may be due to the need to attach a diopter correction lens. It is also worth making sure that the eye-piece glass is free from dirt and grease.

Q. The viewfinder display appears but then disappears from view.

A. If the camera is not held level, the display may not be visible when our eye is looking straight ahead. Use this as a rough guide to determine that the camera is being held straight.

The Body Control Points

Now let us return to the other control and feature positions on the outside of the camera. Start with the hot-shoe on top of the camera.

The hot-shoe is the latest in terms of Nikon design. On it we can see four contact points and at the top (camera facing away from us) a small hole. This hole is part of what Nikon call the "Posi Mount" system. In layman terms a pin from the base of either the SB25 (discontinued) or SB26 flash units slots into this hole to make a secure grip when the locking screw of the gun is turned. A simple but incredibly effective way of making sure the contact between camera and gun is, well, ... positive. Why did they not do this years ago?

Anyway enough of my irrelevant comments. Chapter 5 explains what the contact points do and explains the incredible way the F70/N70 controls flash illumination.

On the side of the prism is a small button. Press this once and the built-in flash unit - Nikon call them speedlights - pops up and instantaneously starts to charge. The flash will fire whenever the unit is in this up position, so press down on it to disengage the speedlight.

On the top-plate but still on the left of the camera we see four buttons. Two are painted in yellow with the words OUT on one and IN on the other. We have already mentioned how to use the OUT button to reset the F70/N70 to its factory set features. It is also possible to program the camera with up to three sets of alternative reset modes where the camera returns to one of these by pressing the OUT button as before, but this time setting a number between one and three. This is called the Quick Reset Feature. It is at this point however that we need to confirm what the other buttons do and how the information about the settings they make are shown on the top-plate L.C.D..

Function Button

Below the OUT button is a button curved in shape marked with the word FUNCTION on it. This is the button that we need to depress and hold down while turning the Command Input Dial, so we can set one of the camera's features ready to be changed.

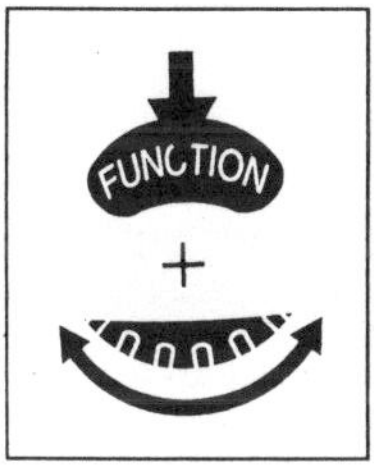

Try this. Press and hold the FUNCTION button down. While doing this (with the camera switched ON) rotate the Command Input Dial and notice how a small triangle moves around the base of the green area of the L.C.D. panel. With each turn of the Command Input Dial the triangle or pointer moves adjacent from one of the boxed sections above it to the next. If we leave the pointer at any one of these boxes and release our finger, we have set that box ready for a change to be made to its contents. For this second step we need to use the SET/Self-Timer button.

SET/SELF-TIMER BUTTON

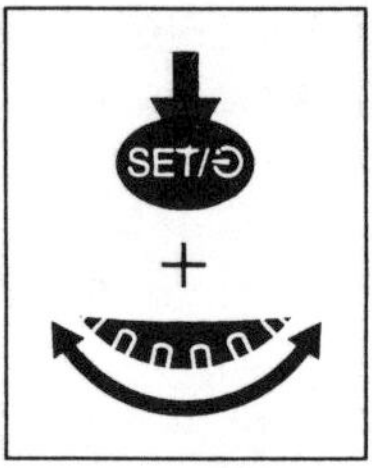

This is dual purpose control. If pressed, without us pressing the FUNCTION button previously, we enter the Self-Timer control. A symbol the same as the one on the button appears in a semi circular section below the green section on the top-plate L.C.D.. It pulsates. We need to rotate the Command Input dial in either direction once to select the Self-Timer feature. If we then release pressure from the SET/Self-Timer button the Self-Timer symbol remains but becomes steady. A press fully down on the camera's shutter release button will give a 10 second delayed action before the camera fires which can be cancelled at any time by turning the F70/N70 off. The delay time is not changeable like on some cameras. When the Self-Timer sequence is in motion a red L.E.D. pulsates on the camera's front grip. As the last second is reached it becomes steady. If we set the camera to its BULB setting then the Self-Timer exposure is made at around a 1/30th of a second at the "F" stop size set. All auto exposure modes work out the exposure for themselves, while in Manual mode we have to pre-set the correct exposure.

More often however this button will be used directly after the FUNCTION button, as it is this SET/SELF-TIMER button that we hold down to enable us to rotate the Command Input Dial and change the features in the box that the pointer is active in.

I am sorry to say that I think Nikon have pandered here to the "gadget freak brigade" with this sequence of events. To be frank I have set the self-timer often when the camera was new when trying to change a function in a box as this sequence is not a logical one. The F90/N90, F801/N8008 and F601/N6006 series of cameras also use push down buttons and a Command Dial, but they work very well with just one button held down and the Command Dial rotated, not a two stage sequence of the same thing! In absolute honesty, however, I have become used to the F70/N70 methods and no longer make such mistakes, but I wonder how many potential customers have made the same mistake as I did and have therefore looked at other cameras, believing the F70/N70 to be complicated? In real use I find it best to use the pressure from the thumb on my left hand as if a rocker switch was underneath it. Heavy pressure forward controls the FUNCTION button while a shift in the pressure enables the SET button to be used without removing pressure completely to move from one to the other.

In/Out Buttons

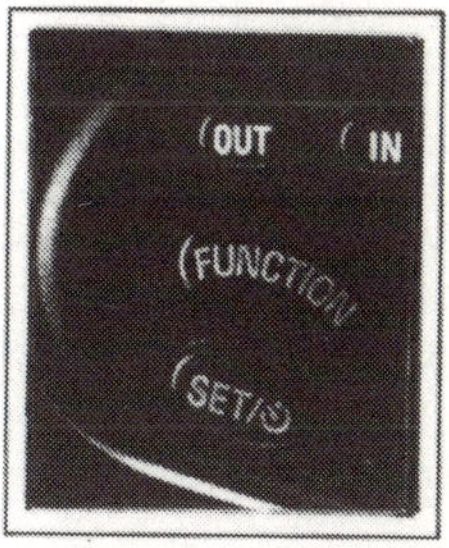

Above the FUNCTION and the SET/SELF-TIMER buttons are the IN and OUT buttons marked in yellow. The OUT button was briefly mentioned before but lets take a closer look at both it and its sister button marked IN.

Let us presume for an example that most of the time, particularly if the camera is new, Programmed exposure mode, 3D Matrix metering, DX Coding and other automatic settings are used. As we become more familiar with the camera we will hopefully move on to more controllable settings. The idea of the IN button is that once we have set the camera to the Programmed mode and the other features we use as standard, we then allocate those features a number either 1, 2, or 3. We do this by setting the camera to those features we most often have in operation. Then, while holding down the IN button and rotating the Command Input Dial, we can set a reference number in the yellow box of the top-plate L.C.D.. It is up to us if we choose the number 1, 2 or 3. They appear in sequence, so that once we have turned the Command Input Dial in one direction we reach either number 0 or 3. Turning the Command Input Dial further in the same direction will not change the number any more. We have to rotate the opposite direction of the turn to go towards the other numbers.

We can of course set up to three different combinations, but to be honest I cannot really see an individual using three exact combinations that often. Having said that, there is another reason for having such a wide choice and a very sensible one at that. Let us presume that, rightly or wrongly, as the owner of this fine machine you have the most knowledge about its operation within your family. You can therefore set up one of the QUICK RECALL modes to your preferred settings. As an example Aperture-Priority exposure, Spot metering, Wide AF and - 1/3rd E.V. Exposure Compensation which you may prefer if you are a transparency user.

The benefit of the QUICK RECALL feature is that you could set a fully automatic set of controls - Programmed Exposure, 3D Matrix metering Wide AF for your partner if they are not as comfortable with a camera and add to that, say, Flexible Program instead of normal Program for a friend as the third option. This will also be useful in, for example, situations where the camera will be a pool camera. Many Police forces for instance equip ordinary officers at certain times with a camera. If the first thing they always did was to dial in a number of a selection that was point and shoot - fine, no need for an in depth knowledge of a product that they may not use every week. I seriously recommend that we do not get carried away with setting all three for our own tastes as it becomes difficult to remember which number refers to each combination when we do not use this feature for some time. Fine, once again, for those who want to play with buttons, but not those of us who want to create images.

Film Rewind Button 1

The IN button also doubles up as one of two rewind buttons. Marked in red just to the right of the IN button is a film rewind symbol. The IN button must be pressed for about a second simultaneously with the other rewind button on the other side of the top-plate (PS button). We can

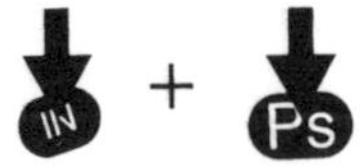

then let go as we have activated the rewind sequence which stops itself upon completion.

I have found that on more than one occasion I have tried to rewind the film but have found that I have had to press the buttons on a number of occasions to get the sequence to operate.

There is one very nice point about the F70/N70 and film rewind however. That is the noise, or lack of it, particularly when we set the silent rewind feature. We look at this later on. On completion of the rewind sequence the word END shows top left of the top-plate L.C.D. and in the middle of the L.C.D. of the viewfinder.

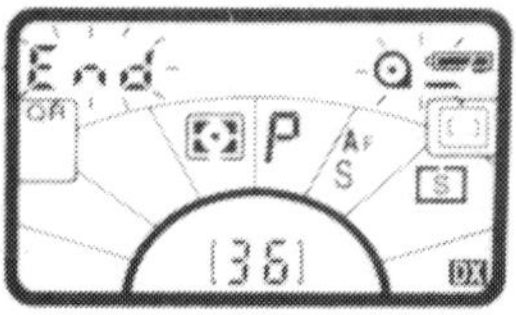

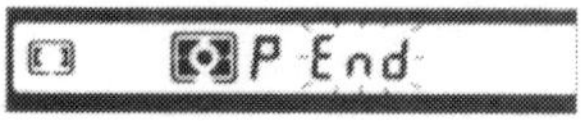

Now we have covered the left of the F70/N70 top-plate let us move to the right-hand side. I think you will agree that the left side is uncluttered and straight forward in its operation. The right is more congested but, as we work through them, all will become clear.

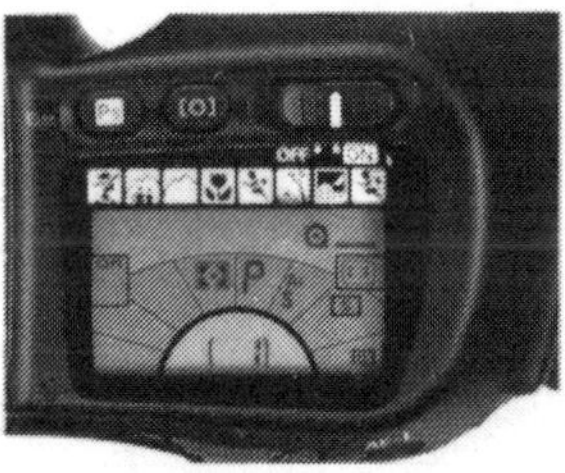

This side of the F70/N70 is dominated by an L.C.D. panel. On it is displayed an incredible amount of information, but here again I have a gripe! It is not, to me anyway, the large, clear, easy to read display Nikon claim. It is at times, I suspect, very difficult for some people to see all of the small symbols and letters because too much is shown in too small a space. Once again however, practice does make assessing it easier. We will first of all take a trip around the remaining control buttons that bring different settings to life on the L.C.D. panels.

Ps (Vari-Program) Button

On the right of the prism forward of the top-plate is a button with a white background with the letters Ps painted on black on top. This is the button to enter and select one of the special program modes of the Vari (Variable) Program list. If you press and hold this button down and rotate the Command Input Dial look below the small black on white pictograms at the top of the L.C.D. panel. Below them is a small pointer that moves along the row of different boxes, each indicating one of the Vari-Programs. The Ps button is in the same colours as the Vari-Program symbols as a colour coded control match.

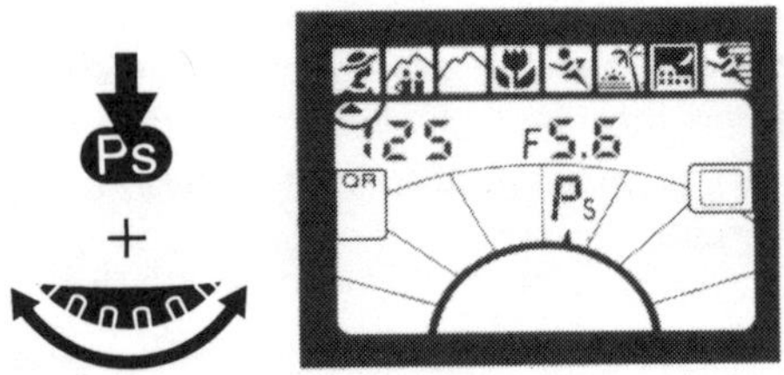

Film Rewind Button 2

The Ps button doubles up as the second rewind button. Film rewind starts when it is simultaneously pressed with the IN button.

Autofocus Detection Area Button

This is a button whose indication is marked in blue on a black background. The effect of using this button is seen in the small blue box on the L.C.D. panel. We can choose Wide Area AF which is indicated by the same oblong jaws as seen on the top-plate or Spot Area AF which is the small circle, again as seen on the focusing screen. To set either we have to press the button down and rotate the Command Input Dial until our setting shows. If we

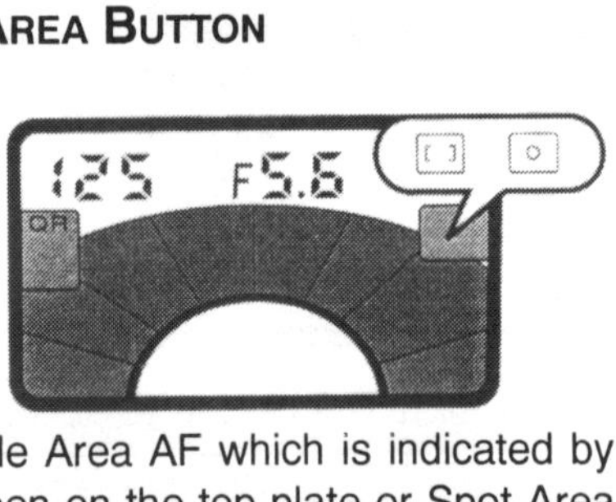

continually rotate the dial the display alternates between the two.

ON/OFF BUTTON

This button was mentioned earlier in the beginning of this chapter.

THE LIQUID CRYSTAL DISPLAY

This is the major information centre of the camera. It displays all relevant shooting data, not just the major aspects as on the viewfinder L.C.D.. Getting to know this panel like the proverbial back of your hand will pay dividends in the time that you won't lose reaching for instruction books. I can't pretend that it is the easiest Nikon display I have used, but the bottom line is that it is usable to the degree that looking in the right place becomes second nature. Later chapters describe the way each feature operates and the effect that results. But first we take a walk around the display.

A green centre section dominates the L.C.D.. It is here that the operating modes are displayed. Below this is a semi-circle in which we only ever see either a frame count or the self-timer symbol if this has been set.

Sandwiched between the green section and the Vari-Program indications is a clear part of the L.C.D. in which the "F" stop and shutter speed is shown, when and only when we have pressed the shutter release gently or taken a shot. When the display in the viewfinder shuts off after 8 seconds, so does the "F" stop and shutter speed indication. When we turn the F70/N70 on we see those features that were last active displayed in the green panel. If we then touch the shutter release, the "F" stop and shutter speed appear.

The Green Zone

This is an area that can have a number of features active at any one time. The area of the green zone is divided into small boxes which stay blank if the feature that they indicate is not in use. We will start at the left and work around the eight sections in which are indications that different features are in operation. The characters are in black on a green background or very occasionally green inside a black box.

Box 1 - Automatic Exposure Bracketing

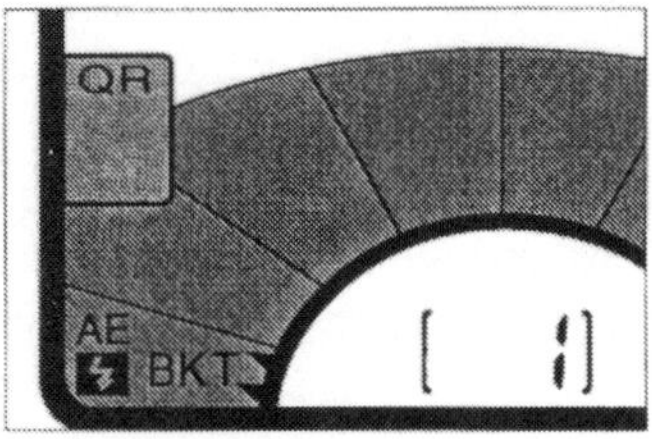

This box shows us when we have set a bracketing sequence for either daylight photography or photography with flash, the built-in flash or a TTL dedicated one. When we are using this feature for flash a lightning bolt symbol appears with the letters BKT (bracketing) next to it. The lightning bolt disappears when we are using just bracketing and daylight. If the box remains empty, no bracketing sequence is activated.

Box 2 - Exposure Compensation With Daylight Or Flash

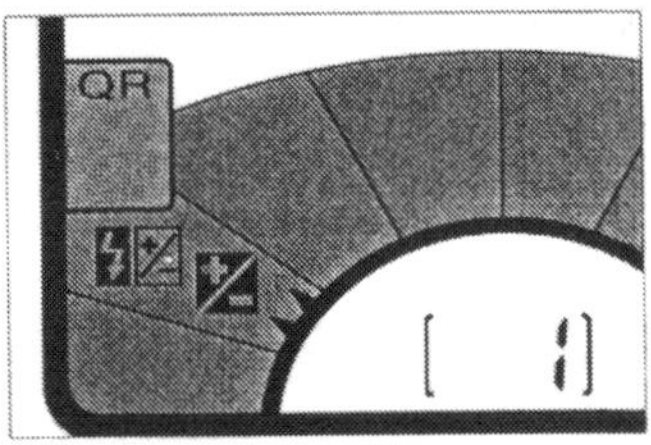

A +/- symbol shows in this box to indicate that we are using Exposure Compensation with daylight. If it is flash illumination that is being adjusted by this feature then a lightning bolt symbol is also displayed. If not in use the box remains empty. Once again a symbol is shown only if we are using this feature.

Box 3 - Flash Mode

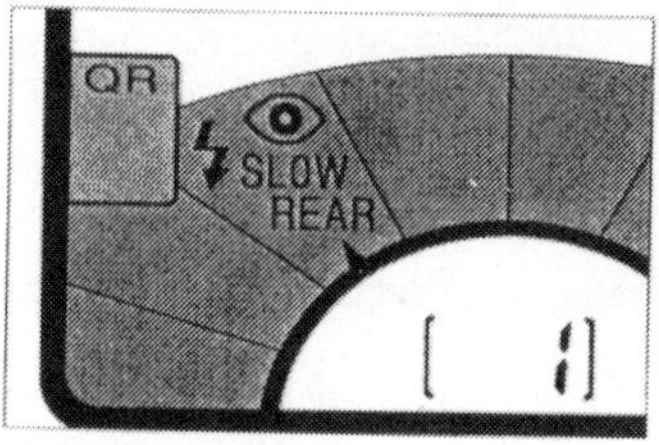

When we select red-eye reduction an eye symbol is shown. For REAR curtain TTL flash we see the word REAR and the word SLOW is shown when slow synchronisation is activated. At other times a lightning bolt is displayed to indicate that normal flash is operating without the other features.

Box 4 - Metering Mode

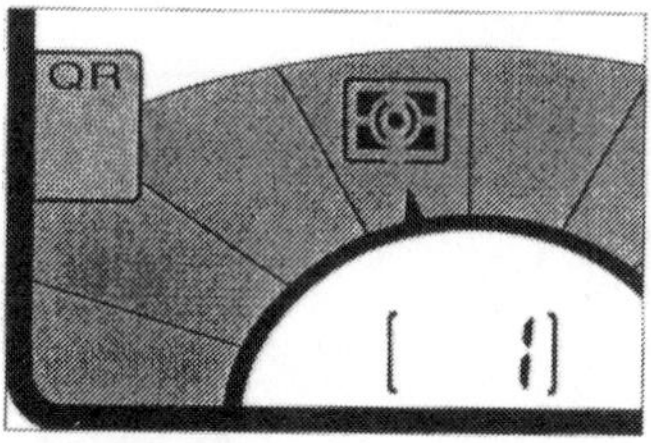

There is always an indication inside of this box as we always will use some form of metering or one will be active. One of three symbols is shown - Matrix for 3D or Advanced Matrix metering, for Centre-Weighted metering a circle surrounded by two small outer lines, and Spot metering indicated by a Spot. These are just the same as the symbols shown inside the viewfinder

Box 5 - Exposure Mode

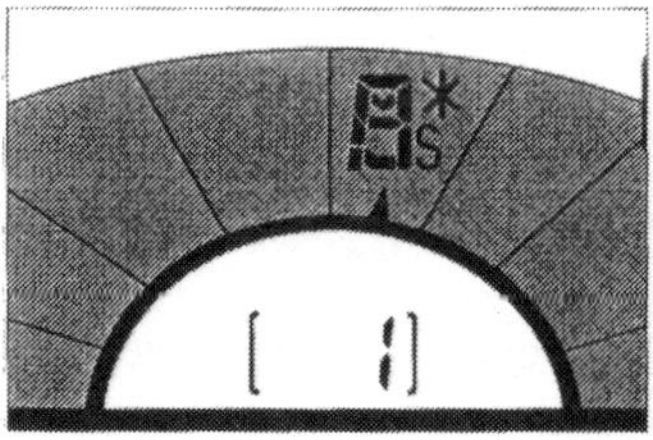

Quite logically the exposure mode in operation will be displayed in the box to the right of the metering box. The letters that appear are as follows:-

Ps = Vari-Program.
P = Auto-Multi Program.
A = Aperture-Priority.
S = Shutter-Priority.
M = Manual.

In addition, when using either of the Programmed modes, a * may also show in the top right of the box. It is the indication that Programmed Shift has been activated.

Box 6 - Focus Mode Indication

If we have set the focus control switch on the front of the camera to 'M' - 'MF' for manual focus appears in this box. If 'A' for autofocus is selected then 'A' is shown. In addition a letter 'S' for autofocus with Single Servo Priority or a letter 'C' for Continuous Servo Priority (what terminology!) will be displayed. They are mentioned in the chapter on autofocus.

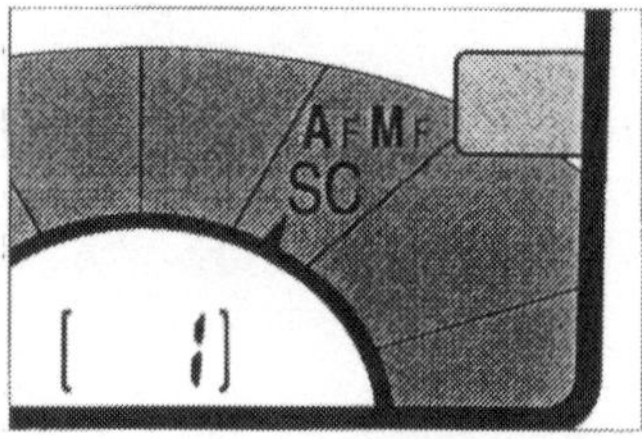

Box 7 - Motor Driven Advance

The rate of film advance is shown in the next box. H = Continuous high speed up to 3.7 frames per second. L = Low speed up to 2 frames per second, while S = single frame advance. In addition the letters SL appear when we decide to have a single frame advance, but in addition this setting indicates that a very quiet rewind will take place when we finish the film........and it is! A very nice touch that means we can use the F70/N70 in many sporting events where before we could not due to the noise.

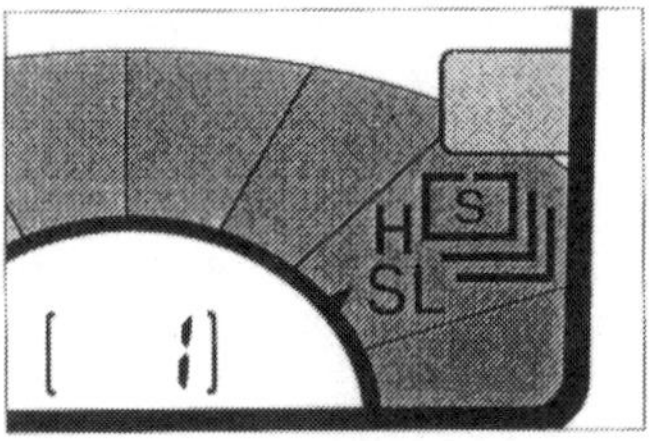

Box 8 - Film Speed Setting

The very last box shows us either the film speed we have set manually into the camera or that the automatic DX coding system has been selected instead after reading a suitable

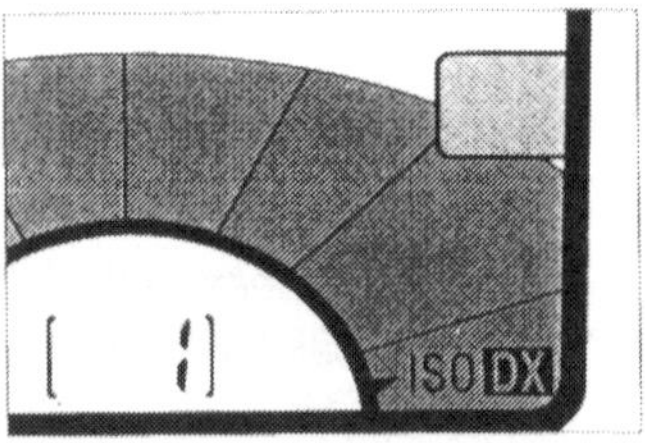

bar code from the cassettes outer. The film speeds that are automatically read by DX coding are 25 - 500 I.S.O.. We can set any of these film speeds manually. In addition we can also set films speeds down to 3 I.S.O. and up to 6400 I.S.O.. Unlike many compact cameras every known speed can be set between the extremes, not just specific ones. So if your tastes are for the unconventional the F70/N70 can cope. If we load a non DX coded film, and have the camera set to the DX coding position, Err and I.S.O. pulsate as a warning that we should set the speed manually.

If like me you have left a film rewound in the camera, the next time you go to use it the film symbol will blink.

This completes the green section. There is a lot going on and I would like to meet the marketing person who calls the symbols large and easy to see. That aside it is very informative!

Shutter Speed and "F" Stop Indications

The shutter speed and "F" stop information is shown above the green section but only when the camera's metering is active.

All that we need to do now is remind ourselves about lens interchangeability and one or two tips along the way.

Changing Lenses

The essence of S.L.R. photography is the ability to select and use different lenses, each with its own characteristics and strengths. The Nikon mount is known as the "F" mount and has remained in the same basic form, with only a few minor changes since 1959. When you think about the progress of technology in nearly every area of human endeavour - that is some testimony either to a chance design or a thoughtful one.

Our F70/N70 will accept any Nikkor lens made since 1981, be they manual or autofocus. We have a chapter a little later on that will give some useful hints and tips regarding the most suitable choice of lenses. For now though let us run through how to change a lens.

a) With the F70/N70 facing us, look at the lens mount. At the 1 o'clock position on the outside of the mount is a small white spot. This is the lens indexing point. We must match the lens indexing point of the lens to this position in order to start the mounting process or in order to detach a lens

b) If the lens in use is an autofocus type, the chances are that on the back of its mount, one of the retaining screws is black in colour. This is the lens indexing point. Early autofocus lenses and all manual focus optics have no screw coloured black. With such lenses we must look at the focus position line on the lens barrel and imagine that line running to the end of the lens to the mount. We then match this imaginary point to the camera index position. Don't worry it is easier to do than it is to explain it.

   Prior to 1981, manual focus lenses had meter coupling prongs fitted. Unless they have been modified to the A type of fitting THEY CANNOT BE USED ON THE F70/N70! A Nikon service centre will be able to advise.

c) Once we have matched up the appropriate points we should push the lens into the body so the bayonet on the lens becomes the inner mount. Then turn the lens anti-clockwise until a click is heard and the lens can be turned no more. It is a common problem that people new to Nikon do not turn the lens fully and therefore the contact points between AF lens and camera body do not meet properly. I have yet to meet anyone who has turned the lens too hard when mounting it, so don't be too gentle, but obviously if in any doubt stop.

The Rest Of The Body

There are some other parts of the body that need commenting on. The first point is the large indent on the camera's back that acts as a thumb pad. This is a nice touch and comfortable. On the opposite end of the camera back is a Judas window. This shows us if a film is loaded and the outer part of the cassette. On the inside of the back are some light tight seals that stop any light affecting the film through this window.

Automatic Exposure Lock Button

This button is situated on the camera back near to the Command Input Dial. When using any of the auto exposure modes - Programmed, Aperture-Priority or Shutter-Priority, the camera's exposure is maintained at whatever level that was appropriate when the button was pressed. If we change the composition and/or the lighting level changes, the exposure is still made at the locked value. But - oh dear! What a disappointment! This button is next to useless! The position of it is fine, but unlike some other makes, Nikon require us to keep our finger on this AEL button all the time if we want it to be active. It is too flimsy and very difficult to keep pressure on. With gloves on this becomes a very frustrating experience. The bottom line is that this feature I find very important, but with the F70/N70 very unreliable! It is surely more practical to allow one press to activate the lock, while another cancels it. A viewfinder symbol should then appear if the exposure is locked.

On the base of the camera is a standard tripod bush, while on the front below the F70/N70 logo is a cover under which is a two pin remote control socket. We can fit electronic, radio or modulated light releases into this socket. More on these in the chapter on accessories.

Finally, at each end of the camera is a lug to fit a whole variety of Nikon or independent straps to. While on the subject, there is normally very little to say about camera straps. However I have been using (on my medium format system) a superb Op/tech strap and highly recommend them for any camera, as they do help reduce the apparent weight of the camera - although the F70/N70 is far from heavy.

Loading The F70/N70

The camera back, once opened, reveals the empty cassette chamber into which we slip the film canister. The canister fits with the writing on mostly upside down. Part of the film, called the leader, sits outside of the cassette. This should be pulled across to the opposite side of the camera. There is a small orange coloured square at the point that we should slip the tip of the leader beyond. Make sure that the sprocket holes in the film sit on top of the sprockets of the advance symbol. Please be careful not to press on the shutter curtains during loading of the film as they are very delicate.

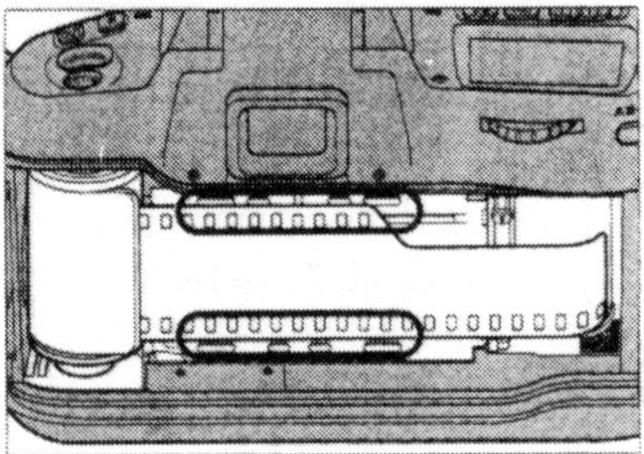

Close the back until it clicks. Release the shutter once and look at the top-plate L.C.D.. 'E' for empty shows if no film is loaded and if the film we attempted to load is not loaded properly. At the same time the film symbol will blink, and the letters "Err" appear. It should be steady when the film is loaded properly.

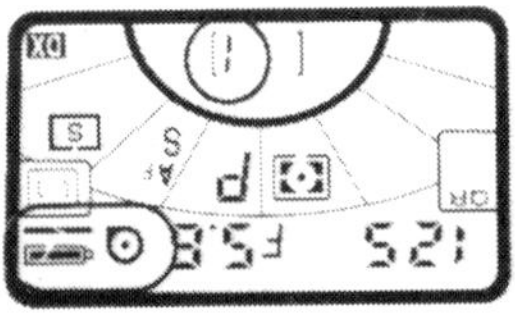

Chapter Two
Creating Memorable Images

Don't let any glossy brochure mislead you. Photography is a relatively simple process. Or it used to be before electronics enabled manufacturers to over-complicate it with a variety of ways to reach the same result. I am not having a swipe at the F70/N70 specifically, because when I start to analyse each of its features there is a good reason for them all, if not for us personally, then for someone else. So before we look at "the means to an end", let us look at the end first.

Light Measurement

During the pioneering days of photography back in the middle to late 1800s, metering to determine the correct combination of "F" stop size and shutter speed was an incredibly hit and miss affair. At best a practitioner's experience enabled him to look at a subject or scene and say .... 2hrs exposure, or whatever exposure was required. We have come a very long way indeed, but remarkably, bearing in mind the progress made, obtaining the correct meter reading and hence exposure is still one of the major causes of failed amateur pictures (plus more than a few professional ones as well).

Like all modern cameras the metering systems of the F70/N70 works by reacting to the light that has come from the subject/scene through the lens (TTL). The metering system is housed inside of the camera's viewfinder and faces the focusing screen.

When we consider how sensitive the systems are we are quoted this in E.V. or Exposure Value terms. An E.V. is a term applied to a particular strength of light. The higher the E.V. number, the brighter the light.

E.V. enables us to select an "F" stop and shutter speed combination that will give the correct exposure. But as an

E.V. measures the strength of illumination, a number of different "F" stop and shutter speed settings can all equal the same lighting strength, and correct exposure can be used. As an example, E.V.1 is a shutter speed of 1 second and an "F" stop of f1.4. But it is also 2 seconds at f2.8 or 1/2 of a second at f1.2 as just 3 examples.

There can be differences in the E.V. range that different metering options, called patterns, operate at. This is mentioned with each section on each method.

When considering the F70/N70, we have three different but more than capable metering options. Negative (print) film also has an in-built safety against poor exposure called exposure latitude. So what are the characteristics of each of the three metering patterns?

3D Matrix Metering - The Best To Date?

This is one of Nikon's favourite sons. For over a decade Nikon have led the field when it comes to developing automatic metering systems that are supposed to work out the meter reading for a correct exposure, in the way that an experienced pro would. That at least is the claim!

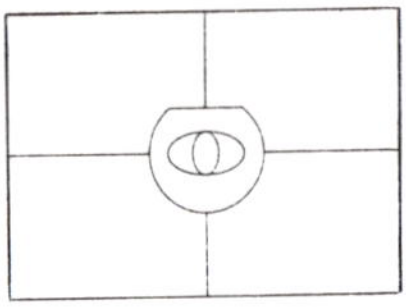

To do this, the following basic diagnostic principles are applied. First the metering cell which is placed inside the camera's viewfinder measures the light reflected off of the focusing screen. The metering cell is made up of small and individually sensitive areas or segments as seen in the accompanying diagram. There are 8 in total in the F70/N70.

Each of these segments measures the amount of light from a different portion of the subject/scene. The reading is interpreted by the camera's computer to determine the strength or brightness of the reading. This is the first denominator to 3D Matrix metering.

The second factor is this. Once all of the brightness values from each segment are known, it is possible for the camera's computer to determine the contrast of the subject/scene by comparing the brightest and darkest parts. Contrast is the second denominator the system needs. These two components have been used by Nikon in previous cameras for basic analysis with no other criteria, until the launch of the F90/N90 in the autumn of 1992. Then a third factor, hence the term 3, was added. That was 'distance information' or as the company has christened it - 'distance technology'.

What distance technology does is quite simple. Each "D" type lens is made with a new type of electronic chip that tells a suitable camera exactly upon what distance it is focussed. A pre-programmed series of controls then switches off, in effect, the reading from some of the segments if the focused upon distance is not infinity or a very great distance. This starts with the very outer segments moving inwards as the distance focused upon becomes shorter. So what is the rationale behind such a technique?

As we focus on a subject at progressively closer distance, the magnification of a subject on film gets larger. If we take the example of a flower - filling the frame with most of it means that the reading from the very central reading segments is important as they cover the subject. If, as is often the case, a small amount of background that is not the flower is within the frame, this is irrelevant to our calculation. In the majority of pictures taken, particularly at close distances, we centralise the subject. Therefore the F70/N70 only uses the central segments for a meter reading - quite logical really.

At the other end of the distance scale, the subject can potentially come from a large area, therefore all eight segments are analysed. There are of course many in between combinations.

Once the computer on the F70/N70 has carried out the above assessments, the information on scene brightness levels and whereabouts are analysed. Thousands of "pattern matches" exist in the computer's memory to twin the reading to. Each of these "blue prints" contains an adjustment where needed for an exposure that will give a better result than a traditional Centre-Weighted meter reading.

For the concept alone Nikon probably deserve more credit than they have received for Multi Pattern metering. But the question that is probably running through your mind is - does it work? The answer is yes ..... and no.

Initially the concept was devised for those people who were new to photography or still had a limited knowledge of metering. That has remained one of the major factors behind the idea. As with many ideas designed for amateur photography however, what at first was scorned by professionals was later to be taken into their armoury of options. The professional who works with rapidly changing circumstances where there can be no second shot - sports and photojournalism - finds a high ratio of hits with this system. Those who use colour print or black and white can use it with confidence in its abilities to determine a good exposure requirement most of the time. The 3D Matrix is also the best system I have used so far for transparency film.

But to be fair to any make of camera that uses such a system, ultimately it can only be as good as the work that the designers have put in and can only give a technically accurate result.

Q. Is a technically correct result not what we want?

A. In many instances yes. But photography is often about creating moods and feelings. These are sometimes achieved more easily by adjusting metering and exposure to provide an aesthetically pleasing image and not a strictly technically correct one.

I have found that occasionally Caucasian skin becomes overexposed when print film results are returned back from the lab. This is more often than not due to one of two things. First we may have used flash. Most of the Japanese made systems I have seen prefer a slightly stronger effect with flash than I and many others prefer. More on this in the flash photography chapter. The second reason is that the fast automated print machinery used today can get it wrong, even though there may be more than enough information on a negative to give a better result.

Advanced 8-Segment Matrix Metering

3D Matrix only operates when we have a "D" technology lens fitted. If we have an AF or AIP Nikkor having no distance technology incorporated, then only Advanced 8-Segment Matrix will operate. Interestingly enough this is still superior to the 5-Segment Matrix found in the F4, F801/N8008 and F601/N6006 etc..

It seems to me a slight inconvenience though that the same symbol is displayed on the L.C.D. panels for both forms of Matrix. Surely Nikon haven't presumed that everyone who had AF or AIP Nikkor lenses have swapped them all at the same time for "D" type lenses?

Setting The F70/N70 For 3D or 8-Segment Matrix

As with most features there is a two step operation to setting the camera.

1) Press and hold down the FUNCTION button and turn the Command Input Dial until the pointer is inside the metering box. The metering symbol should pulsate for around 7 to 8 seconds.

2) Release pressure from the FUNCTION button while the symbol is flashing and transfer it to the SET button. Then turn the Command Input Dial until the Matrix symbol

appears inside the metering box. Release pressure. Matrix is now in operation.

Q. How do I know if 3D Matrix or 8-Segment Matrix is operating?

A. If the lens you have fitted is one that incorporates "distance technology" you will obtain 3D Matrix. If the lens is an AF or AIP type without "distance technology" then an advanced 8-Segment Matrix operates.

Q. Can I switch between 3D and 8-Segment Matrix?

A. Only if we swap a "D" lens for a non "D" type as in the previous question.

More about 3D and 8-Segment Matrix metering

The system mentioned above operates not only for daylight pictures by themselves, but also in any light source that is continuous, such as tungsten lighting. There may be however a shift in the colour balance of the result, as there can be with fluorescent lighting. In the section on accessories we will talk about colour cast in the section on filters.

When a dedicated TTL flash unit compatible with the F70/N70 is used, the Matrix system selects an exposure to give a good exposure for the existing light, just as it would normally do. The computer in the camera then controls the output from the flashgun to give an exposure of a similar level. The shutter speed that Matrix chooses can vary, so Chapter 5 talks about TTL flash.

Q. Can I get Matrix metering with accessories such as extension bellows?

A. Unfortunately not. It would be possible to make a mechanical link to activate Matrix when accessories not having a C.P.U. are fitted. However as this costs more (as an example the F4) Nikon decided to omit such a feature. Unless the unit has a C.P.U. with distance technology there cannot be Matrix metering.

Q. Are there any circumstances where Matrix is not recommended?

A. Contrary to what the brochure says, yes I think there are. The first is when there is no need to use a clever evaluating system. For instance, a tightly framed head and shoulders portrait will not need it, as Centre-Weighted or Spot metering will cover the subject anyway. In addition I think any form of clever metering is the worst possible thing to use if we really want to learn about metering and exposure - Why? Because we do not know what the camera has or has not done to adjust the meter reading unless we constantly adjust metering patterns to view the L.C.D. panel information. While we could flit back and forth from Matrix and another metering option this can mean that we make the presumption that the Matrix reading is our benchmark. Maybe that is not a bad idea, but traditionally people have used Centre-Weighted metering and learned from their mistakes. I don't think you can beat this tried and tested method, if you have the inclination and patience!

Occasionally I can see that we may be better suited by using the Spot metering option with very wide angle lenses. For example, if we have a distant subject but also have a great range of contrast in the frame, we can pin point the actual subject with the Spot meter.

The other main claim about the system is that the need to use Exposure Compensation or the Auto Exposure Lock button is avoided, making the system point and shoot - just what many people want. The metering range of both Matrix systems is E.V. -1 to E.V. 20.

If we have fitted a lens that is not compatible with one of the Matrix meters the Matrix symbol pulsates on the top-plate

L.C.D.. We can still take pictures but the F70/N70 defaults to Centre-Weighted metering.

Centre-Weighted Metering - Traditional And Time Proven

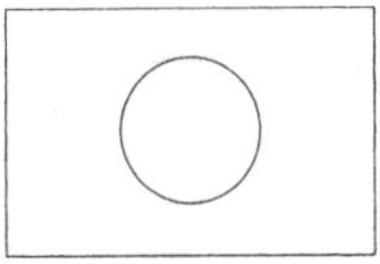

Maybe the Centre-Weighted metering option lacks the glamour that surrounds the other two options. It is an old and well established method of in-camera metering. When we look at the focusing screen we can see, amongst others, a large circle in the middle of the screen. This is the area from within which the meter reading bases 75% of its sensitivity. The remaining areas only have 25% of an input into the reading.

This is quite a sensible ratio that even a few years ago would not have been seen except on the top professional Nikon. As a company, Nikon used to use a bias of 60%/40%. The tighter reading from the centre makes it extremely useful for portraits of any subject that is predominately centralised. While initially in-built camera metering took a reading equally from the entire screen, this soon became more centre-weighted as that was the preference for general use composition. Such systems also reduce the sensitivity towards the top of the frame when the camera is held in the horizontal format, as it is often the sky being so bright that misleads the meter.

Sadly for this pattern it is sometimes necessary to use the Auto Exposure lock button if we have our main subject off centre. I say sadly only due to the difficulty in using this button.

Setting Centre-Weighted Metering On The F70/N70

The metering symbol for Centre-Weighted metering consists of a circle surrounded by two small outer half circles.

1) Press and hold down the FUNCTION button. Turn the Command Input Dial until the pointer is within the metering box.

2) Release the pressure from the FUNCTION button. Switch this to the SET button and turn the Command Input Dial until the Centre-Weighted metering symbol appears. Centre-Weighted metering is now in operation.

More About Centre-Weighted Metering

This metering pattern operates with any lens, regardless of being AF or MF. Bellows and the latest extension tubes all operate without any adjustment. The 75%/25% bias brings the F70/N70 in line with the F90/N90, F801/N8008 and F50/N50 series and not too different to the F3 cameras with their 80%/20% system. This pattern is very useful for close-up shots where the subject fills a large portion of the frame. In conjunction with the Close-Up Program it is very useful, but we have to select Centre-Weighted metering as the Close-Up Program is automatically set with one of the Matrix meters. The E.V. metering range is from E.V. -1 to E.V. 20.

Spot Metering - For The Artist

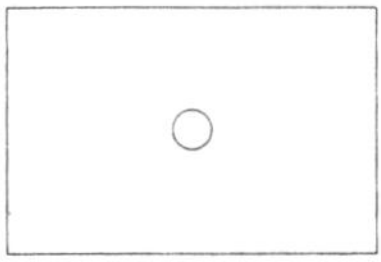

This is my favourite metering mode. A Spot meter is reading from just that - a small spot within the composition. Nearly all of the remaining area is ignored. In the F70/N70 the Spot metering indication is indicated by a small spot on the focusing screen. This is 3mm in diameter. Spot metering can be a route to excellent exposures or a short cut to disaster. It is a metering method that has to be used with quite a few considerations. Unfortunately it is a vast subject that, due to space limitations, we cannot fully exploit in this book. I would suggest that one of the books dealing with the Zone System of metering is worth reading if you wish to explore Spot metering to the full. However I can recommend the following technique that enables a very high percentage of excellent exposures and with a little practice becomes second nature.

The principle behind any metering cell is that it registers the light that comes from the subject in the presumption that the subject reflects 18% of the light that reaches it. The 18% factor is a figure that the photographic industry has taken as its norm. If we therefore point a meter at a subject that has 18% reflectance and all other parts of a camera and lens are working properly, we will obtain a correct exposure. If the other parts of the composition reflect more light than 18% and are therefore lighter, they will appear as such on film. Conversely a darker subject in the same image will appear darker if we point the meter at something of an 18% reflectance. The easiest way to use a Spot meter is to therefore point it at something in the image that looks as if it is a mid tone which roughly equates to 18%.

If we find a suitable portion from which to meter, the film's recording range will give us tones in the final image that are both darker and lighter as well and generally look quite natural. I would especially recommend this system to colour print or black and white workers as these emulsions do have a nice, wide, recording range. If we meter from an area that does not have a mid tone reflection, we can still obtain good images. The area in question will now be reproduced as a mid tone. The other portions of the image will also be affected. We will in effect either be recording more room in the darker or shadow areas of the picture, or more in the lighter or highlight areas. This approach can be used to bring a dramatic change in the way the image is recorded compared to the way we perceive it with our eyes. So Spot metering can be used to reproduce an image as near to the way we see it or with an added dimension due to shifting the recorded range of tone into the shadows or highlights.

Setting Spot Metering On The F70/N70

The symbol used to signify Spot metering is, surprise surprise, a spot.

1) Hold the FUNCTION button down and turn the Command Input Dial until the pointer is inside the metering box.

2) Release pressure from the FUNCTION button and place it on the SET button. Rotate the Command Input Dial until the Spot metering symbol is displayed.

More About Spot Metering

Spot metering is not for those who lack patience and the desire to analyse the results until they have cracked the approach. For those who take photographs only intermittently, I would suggest that Spot metering is best left alone and one of the Matrix systems used. The Spot metering range is limited compared to the other two methods, ranging from E.V. 4 to E.V. 20. Therefore in low light levels the other two metering options will be functioning when Spot metering may have reached the limits of its capability.

Important Points Of The F70/N70 Metering Systems

Regardless of whether we are using Matrix, Centre-Weighted or Spot metering, the F70/N70 display panels warn us if we are outside the metering range for the mode in operation. In any of the automatic modes - Vari-Program, Program, Aperture-Priority or Shutter-Priority the letters LO appear if we are likely to get under-exposure. If the exposure is at the

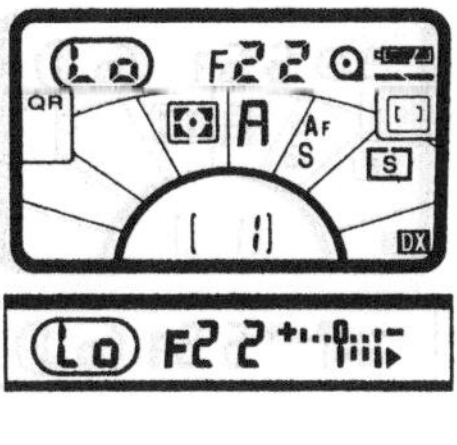

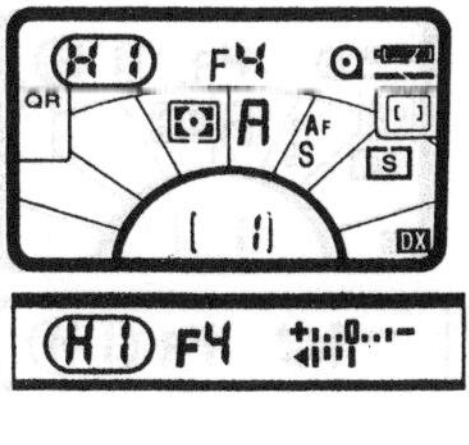

opposite end of the spectrum an over-exposing HI appears. In addition, a bar graph similar to the one shown in Manual Exposure mode also shows. Where the deviation is within 1 E.V., the graph shows this with small vertical lines. Over 1 E.V. and the lines are shown with a triangle pointing away from the display.

If we are using Manual Exposure mode, the whole display blinks on and off if there is going to be an exposure problem resulting from a reading beyond the metering capabilities.

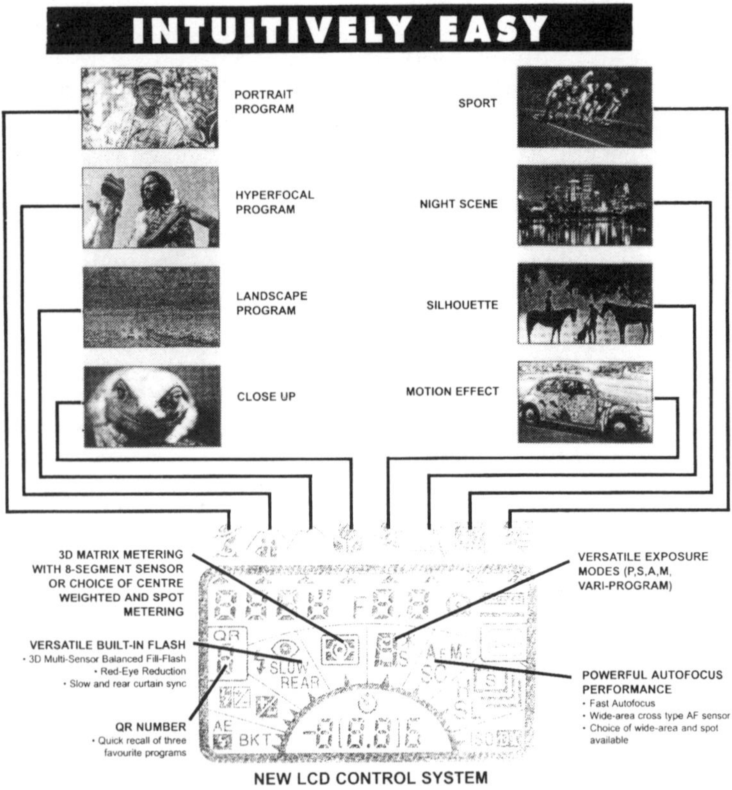

Chapter Three
Exposure - Bringing The Image To Life

If we conceive the idea of the image in our minds and meter for the way we wish to see that image, then the resulting exposure made brings the image to life. We are spoilt by the options on the F70/N70. For some of us we know that we will only use one or two of the exposure modes for 80-90% of our work, but by experimenting with the others, we might just think of a small but important variant on our usual style.

There are a dozen different exposure modes and two ways to manipulate most of them beyond the normal operating parameters. Add to this the incredible flash system options described in Chapter 5 and we have an opportunity for confusion or artistic licence, depending upon our methods of learning and working. Hold on to your seats as this is going to be a trip with lots of turns, curves and bends in the road!

The 12 exposure modes are:-

Manual - We set both "F" stop and shutter speed.

Aperture-Priority - We set our "F" stop size, the F70/N70 sets a shutter speed.

Shutter-Priority - We set our desired shutter speed, the F70/N70 sets an "F" stop.

Auto-Multi Program - The F70/N70 chooses both "F" stop and shutter speed.

Vari-Programs - 8 types each with a specific effect in mind. The F70/N70 sets exposure.

If you wish for my opinion, master the Manual mode and Aperture-Priority and you will have two modes that will cope with all but fast action in a useful manner. Here we now talk about each and every option.

Manual Exposure Mode

The first and, some would argue, the only exposure control worth having. I now use full manual control for probably 75% of my own photography. With it we, and not a computer chip, are in control. Do not let me mislead you though, as to be a real exponent of manual exposure control and do it well does take a lot of practice, but once learnt, what a feeling when we create superlative images!

The two requirements for Manual mode is that we set both "F" stop and Shutter speeds in a combination appropriate for correct exposure. The Command Input Dial when rotated changes our shutter speed in 1/3rd E.V. values. We have a selection ranging from 30 seconds to 1/8000th of a second. In addition we can keep the shutter open for longer than 30 seconds with a cable release and the "Bulb" (B) setting on the F70/N70. Our "F" stop is selected on the rear of each lens.

Setting Manual Exposure:

1) The FUNCTION button should be held down and the Command Input Dial rotated. Once the indicator is displayed in the exposure box, release pressure.

2) Hold the SET button down and rotate the Command Input Dial until a letter M appears on the top-plate L.C.D. panel. The same letter is displayed on the viewfinder read out.

We have now entered Manual mode. A glance at the top-plate will show (if we have gently pressed the shutter release) an "F" stop and shutter speed. A major omission that is made on the F70/N70 is that of a bar graph like that shown in the viewfinder confirming the correct combination, or an indication that we have set the wrong exposure.

Inside the viewfinder we need to adjust shutter speeds and/or "F" stop settings until the bar graph is centralised. Each vertical line that sits either side of the central line is a 1/3rd E.V. step. Count the lines to the side of the central one and we can add up in 1/3rd E.V. the amount we are away from correct exposure. If we see a pulsating display we are outside the metering range of the F70/N70. We can of course continue to make exposures but our own experience is now required. The best way to get the F70/N70 to help is by setting a very much faster film speed into the camera, until a meter reading can be obtained. We can then use simple arithmetic to determine the correct exposure for the actual film speed we are using. Don't forget, every time we double the film speed from the previous one, it is the equivalent of one "F" stop or shutter speed.

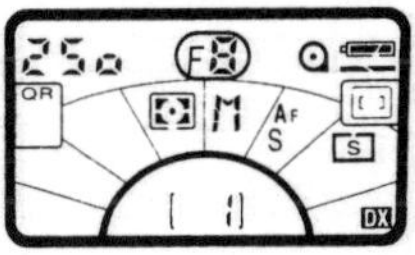

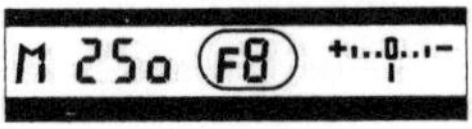

If we are using studio flash we must use manual exposure. Our choice of "F" stop and shutter speed will be governed by a flash meter and not the in-built metering of the camera which is unaware of the studio flash and its effects.

Bulb Exposures

After the 30 second setting the Command Input Dial will show B, which is short for bulb. If we keep pressure on the shutter release after tripping the shutter, the exposure will continue until we release pressure. We need to use a separate meter or guess the exposure but very long exposure times can be obtained. In reality it is better to use an MC12A cable release or a traditional mechanical release via the MR3 adapter. They fit into the remote control socket on the front of the camera below the F70/N70 logo. If you also have an F90/N90 series of camera and the MC20 cable release for that, the MC25 will enable it to be used with the F70/N70.

Q. Why did Nikon not put the MC20 DIN socket on the F70/N70?

A. I have no definite official answer but I presume the cost of the MC20 is prohibitive and therefore the MC12A is preferred. A shame that the MC20 is so much as it is not unknown for a little too much pressure applied with the MC12A to cause the two pins inside the remote control socket to snap off. Be careful therefore. If working in cold conditions warm your hands up or else it is very difficult to fit a MC12A into the F70/N70.

Q. Why do I see the display F_ _?

A. If no lens is fitted or it has no C.P.U., this is the display that indicates that full electronic communication is not happening. Do not worry, the bar graph is the important exposure guide, and works fully.

Q. Why is the exposure bar graph designed to read only one "F" stop either side of the recommended exposure point, when the F801/N8008 and F4 series are two stops?

A. Sadly the space needed to fit all of the other displays into the viewfinder restricts the extension beyond one stop. A real shame as the other cameras have a much more useful display.

Aperture-Priority Exposure Mode

This is I believe the most often used of auto exposure options. We select a "F" stop size that meets with our requirements for depth of field control and the F70/N70 selects the combining shutter speed for correct exposure.

Depth Of Field

Just a little reminder here about a few facts regarding this effect. When we focus a lens it is strictly speaking only focused, and therefore sharp, on one distance. In reality however we can still have different parts of the image in front of and behind this point sharply reproduced as we perceive it. The range that this covers is the depth of field. Depth of field is affected by the lens to subject distance, with the greater depth of field for a constant "F" stop size being at the longer focused upon distances. As an example if we focus at, say, f8 on 5 meters, the depth of field before and after this point will not be as great as when we focus on 20 meters with f8.

If we fit a non C.P.U. lens to the F70/N70, Aperture-Priority is the only auto exposure mode that we can use as a partner to manual mode.

Q. Is it possible to set a "F" stop number between the marked and click stop positions?

A. Yes. This has no detrimental effect on either the camera or lens, while the metering and exposure systems operate quite happily.

Setting Aperture-Priority

1) Hold the FUNCTION button down and rotate the Command Input Dial until the pointer is inside the exposure mode box. Release pressure from the FUNCTION button.

2) Now press down the SET button and rotate the Command Input Dial until A is displayed. Release all pressure - Aperture-Priority is now in action.

I strongly recommend the newcomer to S.L.R photography to try this mode out if only for a few frames on their first rolls of film. To see the effect of depth of field some other cameras have what we call a depth of field preview button. Sadly the F70/N70 lacks this feature, especially strange when it is intended to fill the gap in the market place when all of the

F801/N8008 series have been sold. However, for many, this feature is a little confusing anyway.

When using a TTL dedicated flash unit we will sometimes see the exposure bar graph mentioned for Manual exposure mode. This is an indication not of a totally incorrect exposure, but one that will affect the background of the image. Chapter 5 on flash photography mentions this a little more. However, the same display will show without using flash with the letters 'HI' to indicate over-exposure and 'LO' as an under-exposure warning. If this happens open up the "F" stop size by selecting a smaller number or close the size down by choosing a higher number.

It is always confusing for people to understand why the numbers seem to run against logic. With a larger number set on the "F" stop ring a smaller size is now used. The reason, as with many things in life, is due to the mathematical way at which the numbers are derived. If we took a measurement from the diameter of the front piece of glass in a lens - let us say this is 50mm in diameter, and then divided that figure into the focal length of the lens we would arrive at the number of "F" stop for the lens when used wide open at it widest opening. If the focal length of the lens is 200mm we would get the following:-

200/50 = 4. So that size of "F" stop would be f4.

If we then changed an opening size to one that was smaller - 25mm across we would end up with:-

200/25 = 8.

So f8 is our "F" stop size but the actual opening size is smaller than f4, as in our previous example, which is a wider opening diameter.

Q. Why does the shutter speed indication sometimes pulsate?

A. This is a warning that potentially the shutter speed the camera has to use to match our selected "F" stop, may be one at which we cannot hold the camera absolutely steady. Camera shake may therefore result in picture blur.

The "F" stop is only displayed in full steps rather than 1/3rd steps like the shutter speed, except when we have a variable aperture zoom lens attached or the widest setting of a lens is a fraction of a step like a 50mm f1.8.

Shutter-Priority

For the photographer to whom the shutter speed is of more importance than the "F" stop, this mode offers excellent automatic control. We can set any shutter speed in 1/3rd E.V. steps with the camera automatically adjusting the "F" stop to match our choice. If we photograph action, a technique called panning can help create interesting images. To do this we should pick up the subject inside the viewfinder and follow it from a position where the camera is at a slight angle to one side of our direct pointing forward position. As we swing or "pan" with the subject, keeping it in frame, we release the shutter when the subject is straight ahead, but continue during the exposure and after it to pan the camera in a continuing arc to the other side of the directly ahead position.

Try it with different rates of speed and subject movement and also a range of shutter speeds - it is a way to turn otherwise plain images into more interesting ones.

I recommend Shutter-Priority as well for flash photography. We can then experiment quite easily with daylight fill flash by adjusting the length of the shutter speed which in turn affects how daylight reproduces on film. The longer the shutter speed the greater will be the recording of background detail. In the right circumstances, we can even burn out background detail. When TTL control of the flash is used we can rely on the camera to expose the foreground with flash, with Nikon designing the computer software to avoid over-exposing the subject when long shutter speeds are operative, due to too much daylight and flash together. Like all things though, do experiment as very occasionally I found slight over-exposure occurred.

The range of shutter speeds is quite phenomenal - more than we will really need. In 1/3rd steps the range is from 30 seconds and B for really long exposures through to 1/4000th of a second top speed. Since the 1/4000th of a second facility was introduced to the world by Nikon in 1982 with the FM2, I have needed to use that top speed during the course of working just once. Sure, I have experimented as any creative person should, but in reality I suspect you will find that when you wish to freeze action, speeds of 1/2000th of a second will suffice.

If you intend to use exposure times faster than 1/1000th of a second or longer than 30 seconds it is worth speaking to the film manufacturers about an effect called reciprocity failure. This can mean that to produce a correctly exposed and proper tonal range image, a slight increase in exposure and quite probably filtration are needed. Again though I emphasise that being artistic and shooting without either, you may still find the images work for you!

Setting Shutter-Priority

1) Hold down the Command Input Dial until the pointer is within the exposure mode box. Release pressure from the FUNCTION button and place it on the SET button.

2) Rotate the Command Input Dial until the letter S is displayed. Release pressure from the SET button.

What is the slowest shutter speed that you can hand hold and from which you can get acceptably sharp results for each lens you use? It may be tedious to run a prolonged and specific test, but how about using up those last few frames on a roll to experiment, not only what our own limits are, but also how different ways we hold the equipment may affect it.

As mentioned previously, we have an incredible range of shutter speeds available. On the L.C.D. we therefore see at different times the following shutter speed indications starting with full second exposure times:-

30", 25", 20", 15", 13", 10", 8", 6" ,5", 4", 3", 2.5", 2", 1.6" 1.3", 1 second(s).

1.3, 1.6, 2, 2.5, 3, 4, 5, 6, 8, 10, 13, 15, 20, 25, 30, 40, 50, 60, 80, 100, 125, 160, 200, 250, 320, 400, 500, 640, 800, 1000, 1250, 1600, 2000, 2500, 3200, 4000 fractions of seconds.

If the S for Shutter-Priority pulsates, the lens fitted is not compatible with this mode. We can continue to shoot as the camera defaults to Aperture-Priority.

Auto-Multi Program

This is the mode for the complete novice and the person who really just wants to use the F70/N70 like a compact camera. The F70/N70 will set both the aperture and shutter speed needed for correct exposure. This is a cleverly put together mode as it takes into account automatically the focal length in use, be it a fixed or a zoom option, and adjusts its character accordingly. The camera always tries to use a shutter speed that it is expected most people will be able to hold at, while an aperture is used that will give a reasonable depth of field.

Q. Can I use any lens for Program mode operation?

A. No, only those lenses having a C.P.U. can be used - AFD, AF and AIP lenses.

Q. What happens if I fit a non C.P.U. optic?

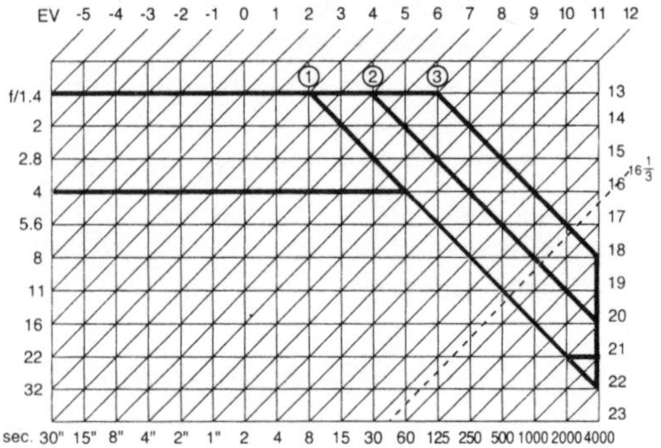

① With a lens shorter than 85mm
② With a 85mm to 199mm lens
③ With a 200mm or longer lens
With AF Zoom-Nikkor 35-80mm f/4-f/5.6 D at 35mm focal length setting
High-brightness limit for Matrix Metering

Program Chart of Auto-Multi Program (at ISO 100)

To check shutter speed and aperture values, follow either the black or grey line to where it intersects the diagonal line.

A. The F70/N70 will fire in Aperture-Priority Mode, F— is displayed on the L.C.D. panels and the letter P pulsates.

Q. Why do the letters FEE replace the aperture reading?

A. The aperture is not set to the orange coloured number. This is required for all programmed modes.

I know one or two professionals who, due to the circumstances under which they work use Auto-Multi Program on other cameras. They do so when the next feature is available - Flexible Program.

Flexible Program

This for me makes a programmed mode a practical feature.

No matter what aperture and shutter speed is chosen by the F70/N70, we can adjust this combination to give a combination more in tune with our depth of field or image freezing ideas. The camera will still allow the same strength of light to reach the film, but in a different combination. Whenever the Flexible Program is activated, a * is displayed next to the letter P on the display panels. We activate Flexible Program simply by rotating the Command Input Dial. We have this combination active until we turn the Command Input Dial further or the meter switches off, or the camera is turned off. Other occasions when Flexible Program is cancelled are returning the camera to the 0 of the QR system, switching to another exposure mode or when a speedlight is switched off or the built-in one is activated or cancelled.

Vari-Programs (Ps)

Regardless what experienced photographers think, the majority of pictures that are shot are by people who do not feel comfortable with the technicalities of the medium. Vari-Programs are an excellent step towards simplifying the creation of images and are at home on this relatively lightweight camera.

The idea is a sensible piece of lateral thinking. Tell a newcomer to photography that they need to set Auto-Multi Program, but for the type of image they want to create they need to use Flexible Program, with the possibility of Exposure Compensation, and they look at you as if you had just spoken Martian! On the other hand tell someone that for a landscape they need to use the Landscape Program and for Portraits the Portrait Program and they are on a much more level playing field as far as their current understanding goes. This is how Vari-Programs operate. I liken this to my learning curve on an Apple Macintosh computer. I knew very little, did not speak the languages of computers, but with an easy start designed for people like me, I am getting somewhere.

There are eight options in the Vari-Program menu. Presumably Nikon have thought long and hard about the eight alternatives so that they cover the majority of interests. The choices as represented from left to right on the top-plate L.C.D. are:-

Portrait Program - A profile of head and shoulders of a lady in a hat.

Hyperfocal Program - A mountain with two people silhouetted in front of it.

Landscape Program - A mountain.

Close-Up Program - A flower.

Sport Program - An athlete.

Silhouette Program - A palm tree against a backdrop of the sea and the sun.

Night Scene Program - A building against a dark sky and moon.

Motion Effect - An athlete with blur lines.

Setting One Of The Vari-Programs:

1) Press and hold down on the Ps button above the top-plate L.C.D..

2) Rotate the Command Input Dial until an arrow appears underneath the pictogram representing the mode we wish to use.

3) Make sure the lens has a C.P.U. and is set to the orange coloured aperture.

In use we should not have to worry about setting shutter speeds and apertures or adjusting an exposure beyond the one the camera sets as this has been accomplished by Nikon's design team. However we can, as experienced photographers, use both Flexible Program and Exposure Compensation if we so wish. Let us take a look at each mode and see what Nikon have designed for us.

Please Note - That on selecting one of the Vari-Programs the F70/N70 is re-set for Matrix metering, Wide area AF (if AF is set), but no Exposure Compensation or Flexible Program, unless we set them ourselves. Some options also use a feature for flash photography called Slow Sync flash.

Portrait Program

Probably the most popular option. A portrait is one of those things that some say a person should be shown in situ, where they work or live or in an environment that is normal for them. Other photographers prefer to record a person in a tighter crop and not have the distraction of the environment they are in. This comes down to personal taste. I think that both have their place. Nikon have however decided to err towards the latter choice. The F70/N70 will select a shutter speed for a handholdable shot. However a wide or large "F" stop is selected as a priority. This will have the effect of minimising the depth of field, making our subject stand out from the background. If we want to increase the effect of a tightly framed image then use, if you have one, a lens with a focal length between 85mm and around 200mm. This gives a reasonable distance between us and the person in real distance but as the above are telephoto in effect they close in nicely on the subject.

Hyperfocal Program

Do not be put off by the name. There is in photography a technique that is used to maximise the depth of field in the image. It is called the hyperfocal distance and although not based entirely on the same technique, this mode goes for the greatest range of sharpness within the image. To get the best out of this mode try including something of interest in the foreground as well as in the distance. Lenses of a wide angle type or even a 50mm lens obtain the greater range of sharpness compared to the longer telephoto effect optics, but once again be creative and experiment. As a matter of course be prepared to use a tripod, monopod or other support as the effect is obtained due to a large depth of field and a small "F" stop size.

Landscape Program

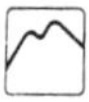

This at first seems a little along the lines of the Hyperfocal Program and it is. I personally cannot see that there was a need for both. Once again smallish "F" stop sizes are selected so sometimes a tripod or steady support will be beneficial. The major difference between the two modes is that the Landscape Program may sometimes select an "F" stop for a slightly reduced depth of field compared to Hyperfocal Program and takes less interest in the top of the image as this is normally the sky. I think this mode will provide many fine images. If using flash don't forget that the flash will only light the foreground - its effect is lost on the background.

Close-Up Program

As the name suggests this mode is for close-ups. Not so much close-ups of, say, a portrait but even closer than that. A small "F" stop is selected to maximise the depth of field, but at the same time to blur the background making the subject stand out. I have in previous books commented that in many close-up shots even greater depth of field is required than that found in this mode with f5.6 and f8 which are typically chosen. My recommendation to you is that a quality tripod is always used and that Aperture-Priority mode is also utilised. That way we can select a smaller "F" stop than this mode and, I feel, get superior images. Any lens that has a macro facility is suitable, but ultimately a Micro Nikkor will be the greatest quality of image production. They are not cheap but can be used for all sorts of photography apart from close-up. My 105mm f2.8 AF Nikkor is one of my favourite lenses, very sharp and great to focus manually. This latter point is important as one area where AF has not proved itself as capable as MF is in close-up photography.

Sports Program

There are no prizes for guessing the type of shot intended with this mode. It is recommended that we do not use flash as if the lighting levels, film speed and "F" stop allow it we can have some very fast speeds available, while switching on a flash would restrict this at best to a 1/125th of a second. That is correct as far as the in-built speedlight and most add-on units. However the SB25 and SB26 speedlights have a special flash mode called - FP. This allows shutter speeds up to 1/4000th of a second to be used.

We can use any focal length of lens but in most situations a longer than normal focal length is better to get in tight to the action. The technique of "panning" as mentioned previously is very useful in sporting photography.

Silhouette Program

I feel this mode is underrated. Its intention is to silhouette the subject against the background. For this we need a bright background and a subject that has both an interesting shape and one that is not as bright as the background. Do not use flash at all as this will counteract the effect. The camera exposes the background correctly causing our subject to silhouette against it. Try if possible to find a subject that has an interesting and distinctive shape. Sunsets and coastal scenes are ideal as backdrops. The reason I like this is that as a technique we can use this when there seems little in the way of conventional images - in bright contrast light such as at midday which is generally thought of as a bad time for normal photography.

Night Scene Program

For many, venturing out at night to take pictures is something not often thought about. It is a shame as bright, man-made lighting, against a black backdrop looks stunning if done correctly. A Cullmann tripod or solid support is a must, as this mode requires a slow shutter speed. There is also a very good case for bracketing exposures and ample opportunity for switching modes and experimenting with progressively longer shutter speeds. Please be careful though as we all know some parts of the world are not the places to be setting up a tripod late at night and flaunting a machine like the F70/N70. I would suggest, as a helpful tip, that you take someone else along, not just company, but an extra pair of eyes in all its meanings. Until you have tried low light or night time photography you cannot imagine how something that looks so ordinary and drab by day, becomes a thing of beauty by night! Flash can also be used to help render a foreground in a beautiful and detailed way.

Motion Effect Program

I am sorry to say that when I first saw this mode on another camera, I laughed for some time. In reality we obtain an image with part of the scene sharp (anything that is stationary) while any moving part is recorded as a blur - something that has ruined countless images due to photographers selecting too slow a shutter speed for the speed of movement. A clever way of marketing the effect don't you think? When using this mode, I re-examined that the use of flash is a benefit as this will still freeze the action at one point (where the flash fires) with a blur as well. Images without flash will of course make the motion effect more pronounced. "Panning" will again play an important role in adding another dimension to the basic theme. By all means try this mode, but for me Shutter-Priority will be more controllable and allow more flexibility for this type of result.

Q. Why is there no Red-Eye Reduction Portrait Program as on other Nikon Cameras?

A. It was thought that photographers using the F70/N70 would rather bring the red-eye reduction control into operation as and when they would like. It can be used with any exposure mode.

More About Exposure

No exposure mode is perfect. There are two other features that are very useful - Exposure Bracketing and Exposure Compensation. Both can be used with daylight or flash photography.

Exposure Compensation

This feature lets us change the exposure for one or any number of shots. We can increase exposure to over-expose or decrease it for under-exposure. We do this by positioning the pointer in the bracketing box via the FUNCTION and SET button.

Make sure that we set just the +/- symbol for daylight and the same symbol with a lightning bolt for flash while holding the FUNCTION button. Then place pressure on the SET button and rotate the Command Input Dial to set our desired amount of compensation. Inside the viewfinder and on the top-plate L.C.D. will appear a +/- sign as an indication until we cancel this feature.

Exposure Bracketing

With this mode we can obtain the exposure as the camera sees it, but either side will be an over- and under-exposed alternative. We choose the amount that the alternatives are different between .5, .7 and 1 E.V. for either daylight or flash. Use the FUNCTION button to set the pointer into the bracketing box and the SET button to set our deviation. The only time we cannot use bracketing is with the BULB setting. A +/- display is shown on both L.C.D. panels and the analog bar graph in the viewfinder moves in the direction of the re-adjusted exposure. If we are using CH or CL drive we should keep the shutter release pressed until the three shots have finished. If we keep pressing the release normal exposures will be made. Exposure Bracketing cancels after 3 shots. It is also cancelled when we turn the camera off.

Are you with me so far? Good, then the next thing to mention is that we can use both Exposure Bracketing with Exposure Compensation. The compensated amount will be added to the bracketing amount

If we are going to use one of the auto exposure modes (not manual) and are not going to be looking through the viewfinder, use the eyepiece cover DK5 to stop light entering the viewfinder and misleading the exposure meter.

CHAPTER FOUR
Focusing - Seeing Is Believing

For a long time camera equipment tests and reviews have homed in on the latest camera's AF capabilities and I think tended a little too often to base their conclusions about the product on this single issue. I think this is wrong as AF is just another feature and not one of any greater importance than, say, the exposure control a camera offers or, for that matter, its ergonomics. The F70/N70 is state of the art as far as AF goes. Indeed as I shall mention it is possibly better in some areas than the famed F90/N90 series.

New Autofocus Module

The Cross Autofocus Module or CAM design used in the F70/N70 is able to take data from both a vertically patterned subject and a horizontal one. It consists of 274 individual CUD elements that read a part of the light reflected from the subject after it has passed through the lens and been directed onto the CAM 274 via a sub mirror.

The information from each of the CUD elements is used by the computer system to determine the focus status - in or out. In the latter, the calculation also determines by how much. The lens is driven to that point accordingly. This is a simplified explanation as in reality the lens is being driven in the direction of the focus position while the computer system still analyses the final stopping position. 274 elements are the highest number of CCDs Nikon have so far used. They provide for a dense CUD array which picks up more information than in other Nikon cameras. In practice this translates into the ability to read slightly finer patterning. That is one of the F70/N70 strong points - arguably it has on this score Nikon's best AF yet. As a comparison the F90/N90 series have 246 CCD elements. Not a major departure I know but a step forward nonetheless. In real photography I think that close-up work will be the type of application that this benefit shows in. This is a good thing as I have yet to find any AF system that can AF in close-up photography to my liking. The F70/N70 is not perfect but is better than previous cameras.

Setting Autofocus On The F70/N70

We have a choice between Wide AF and Spot AF as indicated on the focusing screen. The control button is above the L.C.D. screen on the top-plate. Do not forget to set the focus switch on the camera's front to A.

To select either Wide AF or Spot AF hold down the control button and rotate the Command Input Dial until the representative symbol appears in the viewfinder and in a small blue box on the top-plate L.C.D.. The control button is logically coloured blue as well. In addition there is another option to make. We must decide if we prefer Single Servo AF or Continuous Servo AF. More on them in a while.

Wide Area AF

The width of this detection area is 7mm. This means that around 20% of the 35mm format (width) is analysed for AF detection. The sensitivity is continuous across this area with no "dead spots". At the same time a 3m high section is analysed vertically. Wide AF is most people's first choice but I must say that occasionally its strong point, width of detection, can be a problem. If we have more than one subject in the detection area, the system can sometimes focus incorrectly. The subject with the greatest contrast is locked onto, which is not always what we want. In fairness this seemed to happen less with the F70/N70 than other cameras I have tried. It is not a problem as we can switch to Spot AF or Manual focus.

The real benefit with Wide AF is for action photography where a subject cannot be positioned in the centre of the frame consistently. A typical example would be two

The Nikon F70/N70 Showing AF and Optical Path

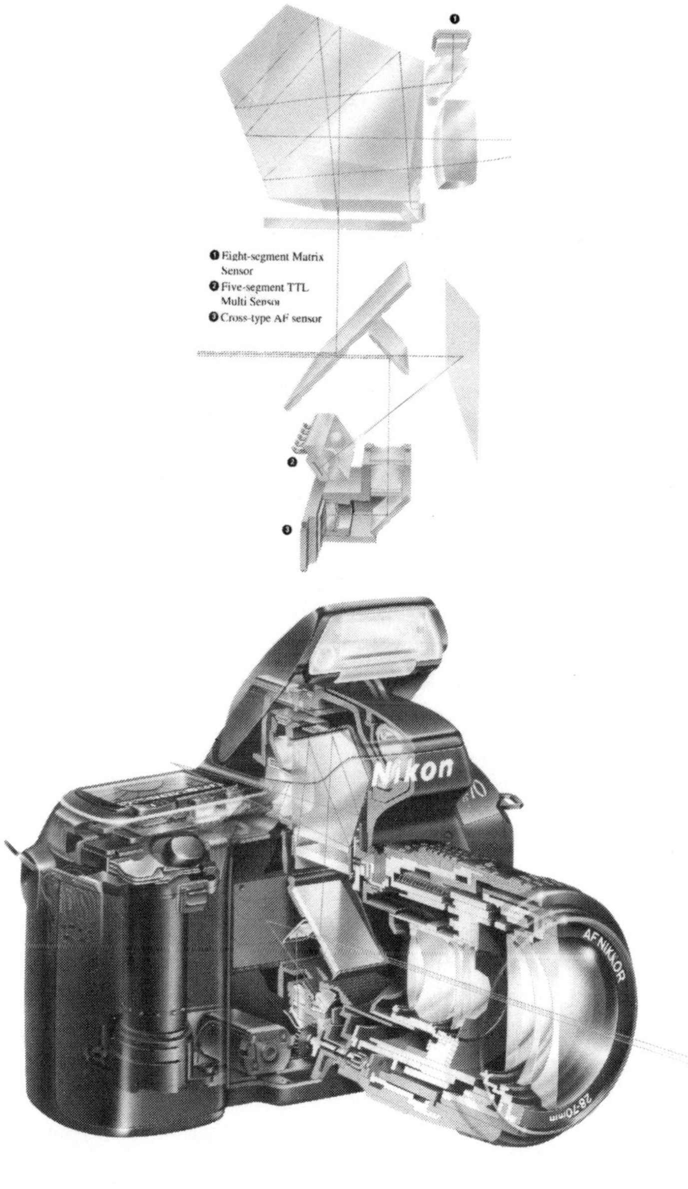

participants together. A Spot AF system will often hit the gap between them and focus at infinity or background.

Spot AF

I like this mode. Due to the E.V. detection range of the F70/N70 being E.V.-1 to E.V.19 it operates in most conditions as does the Wide AF alternative. The time to be careful and switch to one of the other focusing options is when we have the spot covering one tone of colour with little or no patterning on it. The Spot system will not be able to operate in those situations. The chances are that Wide AF due to its larger size will cover different tones.

We now have to decide how we want to control autofocus a step further - either Single Servo AF or Continuous Servo AF. Doing away with the strange sounding terms, what do they mean in reality? Simply this. We can have the camera fire only when the AF detection system has something in sharp focus - Single Servo. Continuous Servo gives us the say of when to trip the shutter. To select one or the other hold the FUNCTION button and turn the Command Input Dial until the pointer is inside the focus mode box. Depending on the current settings, AF with a big letter S or C will show or MF if manual focus is in use on the control switch on the F70/N70's front. Use the SET button and the Command Input Dial to make our selection.

Q. Why would we want to stop the camera from making the decision of when to fire?

A. If we have a fast moving subject (it need not be that fast), the camera may refuse to fire at all in Single Servo AF as it never finds focus due to constant movement. We can use Continuous Servo to take shots after light finger pressure sets the AF system into motion. Exact focus may not be achieved, but we do have the shots.

Q. Why would we want out of focus images?

A. We don't. But if possible use an "F" stop that allows as much depth of field and a suitable shutter speed to stop the action.

In both modes the camera's computer will activate focus tracking automatically, in effect overriding Single Servo AF. Look for the two focus arrows in the viewfinder being constantly displayed as an indication of focus tracking. While talking about the arrows, just a reminder that when they both blink AF cannot operate. If one arrow appears pointing to the left we are trying to focus the lens closer than it is designed to be.

More About Autofocus

For AF to operate we need an equivalent light transmission of f5.6 or wider. We also need a contrast on the subject that is sufficient for the system to determine more than one tone. I find that I still prefer to Manually focus, except when circumstances are constantly changing. The F70/N70 is in the main a step forward in Nikon's AF technology. One annoying thing is however the claim that the AF system is as fast as the F90/N90 series. It certainly is faster than say the Nikon F601/N6006 - I have seen claims that it is 20% faster, but when on Continuous High speed drive and Continuous AF it does not seem anywhere near the speed of its bigger brother. I think that the possible reason for this is the extra CCD elements giving the computer system more to analyse. Certainly the computation speed is faster than other Nikon cameras according to Nikon's own data, but somewhere this seems to be nullified.

Q. How do I lock focus then recompose for an off-centre subject?

A. This can only be done with half pressure placed on the shutter release once the focus has been achieved.

Maintaining the pressure and recomposing does not alter the focus point. However only Single Servo can be used.

Most lenses are driven from a small shaft that rotates from within the F70/N70 body. This matches up to a connecting point on the rear of the lens. You can see this shaft appear and disappear by looking at the camera mount without a lens attached and turning the focus control from AF to M.

The other way to drive autofocus is by having a motor inside the lens with the camera body just supplying the power. The AFI Nikkor lenses work in just such a way. They are fast and very quiet in operation.

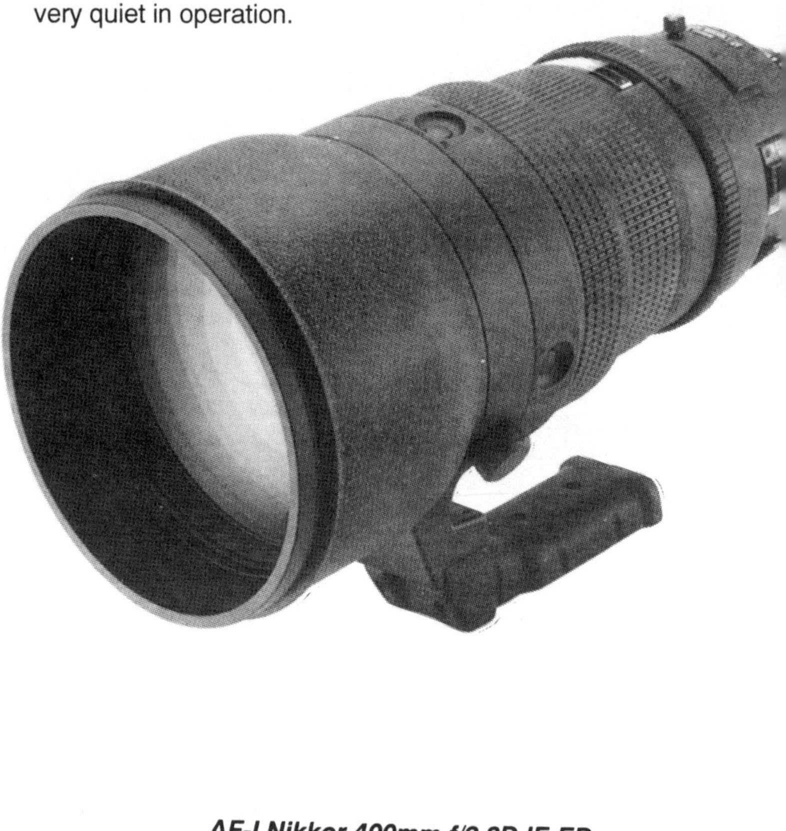

AF-I Nikkor 400mm f/2.8D IF-ED

Chapter Five
Flash Photography

This camera is amazing. It is the most capable of cameras on the market as far as flash photography is concerned for most general uses. This is especially so when we use either the built-in flash or an SB25 or SB26 flash unit which are the latest offerings from Nikon. The F70/N70 shares the same system as that found on the F90/N90 series - a system that has delighted a large percentage of the world's press and sports fraternity. As flash photography is still a cause of confusion for many, we will now take a step by step walk through the options. These are divided into three types of control. Manual, Auto flash or TTL. Each has its merits, but ....

In the Beginning ....

There was only one way to control electronic flash and that was manually. This still has its devotees today and I often use it still, for instance for some of the product shots in this book. The principle is that we put the F70/N70 into its Manual exposure mode, setting an "F" stop and shutter speed that are suitable for the job in hand. We can select any shutter speed up to a 1/125th of a second with the F70/N70, but nothing faster. Whatever shutter speed we use is known as the flash synchronisation or sync speed. If a speed faster than a 1/125th of a second is selected and we are using a Nikon flash unit or similarly dedicated type, the F70/N70 overrides our setting as soon as we turn the flash unit on. What we see is a blinking shutter speed value on the top-plate L.C.D. if it is too fast, while the viewfinder shows the correct and chosen speed of 1/125th of a second.

In order to set the proper "F" stop we need to either take a meter reading from a hand held flash meter or by looking at a chart or L.C.D. panel on the flash unit. Once we have keyed in our film speed, output power we wish to use and, in some instances, the distance between the flash and the subject, the "F" stop we need will be displayed. This sounds quite time consuming but with most applications, where we are going to use one or two flash units, most people prefer to use one of the other two flash control options.

Auto Flash Control

With the need to work quickly in changing conditions came the development of Auto flash control. It is the norm that Manual exposure is used, but it is also possible to use Aperture-Priority if we match the "F" stop on the lens and the same setting on the flash unit. Auto flash uses a sensor on the front of a flash unit that measures the light that comes back from the composition after the flash has fired. As soon as a pre-determined amount has been registered by the sensor, the exposure stops. Like manual flash control, auto flash requires us to set into the flash unit the film speed and aperture. For cameras less sophisticated than the F70/N70, auto flash is a sensible route to follow for point and shoot photography with just one gun.

For the F70/N70 we are spoilt as we have at our disposal a very large selection of Nikon guns which are called Speedlights, and an even larger array of independently made options. Providing they have an I.S.O. hot-shoe they will fit

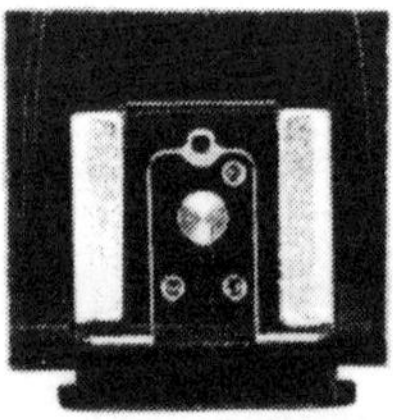

Nikon F70/N70 Hot-Shoe

into the hot-shoe of the F70/N70. Be careful though as some units meant for other makes of camera may have contact points that are not compatible with those of the F70/N70 hot-shoe. If we have such a unit at our disposal, it is better not to connect it into the hot-shoe of the camera but use Nikon's hot-shoe adapter AS15. This has a connection to plug a lead from the gun into the adapter. Most guns come with a P.C. socket into which the lead fits. The same adapter is also needed for the F70/N70 when studio flash is used with a connecting lead.

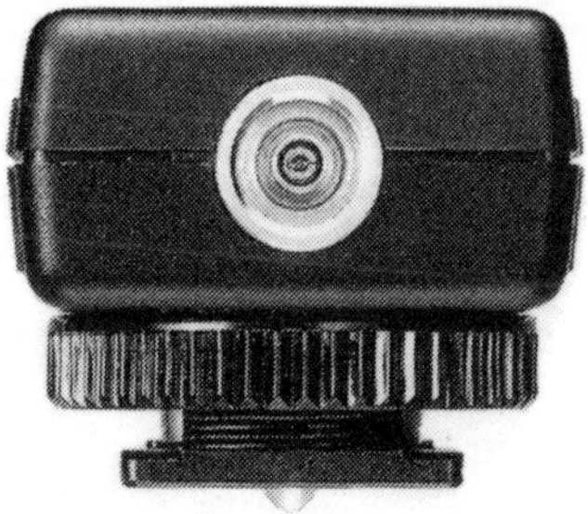

Nikon's Hot-Shoe Adapter, the AS15

The F70/N70 automatically sets the proper sync speed with dedicated units in auto flash mode if they are connected into the hot-shoe directly or via the SC17 TTL lead.

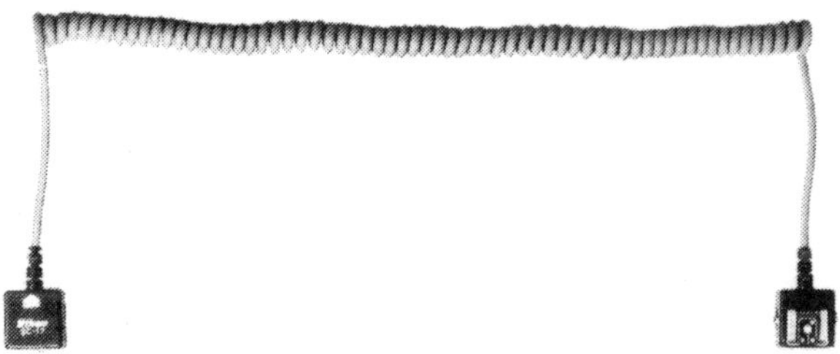

Nikon's SC17 Lead

TTL Flash Photography With The F70/N70

The F70/N70 uses the now common TTL flash control method. The principle is this. As the light emitted from the speedlight hits different parts of the scene, much of it is reflected back into the lens. As the shutter has opened the light passes through the camera and exposes the film. Some of the light however bounces back from the film. A TTL flash sensor facing the film measures the illumination. Once a pre-determined level is reached the flash is quenched. This takes milli seconds or in photographic terms - real time. Any exposure mode can be used, with any light absorbing accessories, such as the 'Sto-Fen' Omni-bounce, as the system corrects for this up to the power limit of the gun. That is common to all cameras but our F70/N70 is far, far cleverer than that.

Take for instance the size of the TTL flash sensor. With most cameras the area measured is the equivalent roughly to the central circle seen on the focusing screen. This is fine but it does not take a genius to realise that if our subject is outside of this area, i.e. off centre, then the sensor will not measure the build up from this, the most important part of the image. We will sometimes get away with this if the subject in the centre that is actually measured is of a similar tone. In addition colour print with its forgiving nature is also a great help. The F70/N70 has a much larger TTL flash sensor that is in fact made up of five segments, like the Matrix meter inside the camera's viewfinder that is used for daylight photography. Once again the segments of the sensor work independently of each other. This means that different parts of the image can be measured at the same time. The first point about this is that if we have a particularly high or low reflectance area this will be ignored as other segments read a more natural amount.

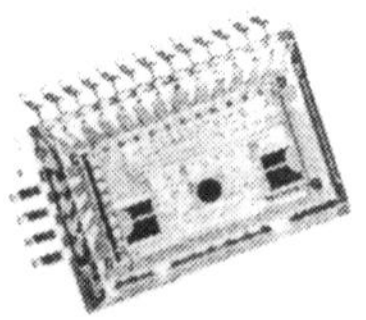

TTL Flash Sensor

As mentioned in the chapter on metering the use of distance technology makes the assessment much easier for daylight photography. The same distance technology also plays a part as well in deciding which segments to use.

So we have at our disposal a metering area that is far wider and more specific than most cameras. The next component plays a very important role whenever the built-in flash or a Nikon SB25 (discontinued) or SB26 are used - a grey 18% reflective shutter.

18% Grey Reflective Shutter

When the flash fires as described, the light returns through the lens. With the two Speedlights mentioned or with the in-built unit in operation, it does this initially with the F70/N70 shutter still closed. The reason? This is in order to establish an even greater accuracy. It helps to determine just before exposure, rather than after it has started, which segment or indeed combination of segments are to be used to measure the exposure. The side of the F70/N70 shutter that faces the lens is painted in a 18% mid grey finish. This directs onto the TTL flash sensor a pre-flash if the built-in speedlight is used, or a series of them if an SB25 or SB26 is in use, before exposure, so a pre-exposure decision can be made. I presume that the built-in speedlight only fires one pre-flash as it is less powerful by a considerable way than the SB25 and SB26.

This is a very simple approach, but some clever person still had to think through the sequence. Where the pre-flashes are concerned, they happen so near to the actual picture taking flash that fires directly after the pre-flashes, that we do not perceive them. If you want to be sure that they are there, then an independent flash meter is required. This will register the pre-flashes. If we then fire the Speedlight on REAR curtain synchronisation the pre-flash sequence does not operate and therefore is not registered by the meter.

Q. When will the pre-flash not work?

A. The pre-flash only works on NORMAL or FRONT curtain synchronisation. It will not operate on REAR curtain synchronisation or whenever the head points in any direction except straight forward (SB25 and SB26). The sequence only operates in the TTL flash mode.

The increased accuracy with the pre-flash is very difficult to quantify, but I have to say that it can, given the right circumstances, be a significant improvement to a system not using it.

The Built In Speedlight

This is an excellent feature of the F70/N70 cameras. I know that Nikon have refused to fit such units into the top of the range cameras, but the convenience of it leads people to use flash more and, in turn, get better images. Why are they not on the pro models?

To activate the built-in unit at any time all we have to do is pop it up by pressing the button on the side of the prism. It

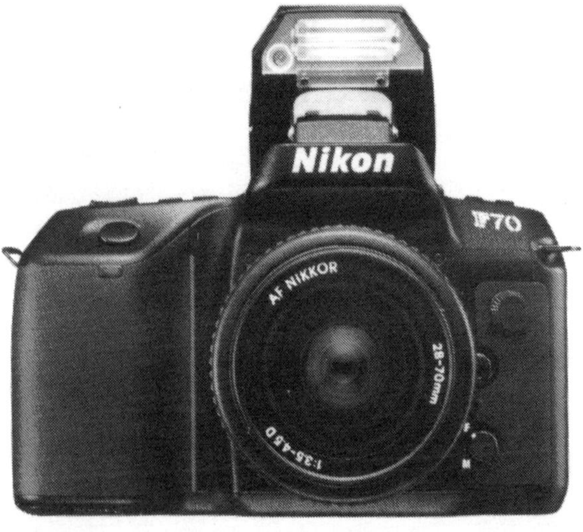

starts to charge immediately with a red lightning bolt shown inside the viewfinder when it is ready. Be sure to leave it a second or so longer if you want to be sure that a 100% charge has been reached as there is a tendency for ready lights to show ready a fraction early. The flash sits at a comparatively high position (around 16mm higher than on the F601/N6006 camera for example), which helps reduce red-eye. To turn it off we only have to push the head back downwards until it clicks. The guide number is 14m.

The front of the head has a plastic diffusing surface. It helps to spread the light to cover a fixed focal length 28mm lens. On the left as we look at it is a small bulb from which the red-eye reduction beam is omitted.

When fired in daylight the flash is controlled to work with daylight not against it. In very bright conditions we can reduce harsh shadows with no more effort than popping up the speedlight, waiting for it to charge and tripping the shutter. The F70/N70 does the rest!

Special Flash Photography Techniques

The F70/N70 has an amazing arsenal of flash photography features. For normal use I re-examined that the F70/N70 is set to normal synchronisation that is indicated by a lightning bolt symbol. We can then use the F70/N70 with the TTL system taking care of our needs and with the pre-flash operative with the built-in speedlight or an SB25 or SB26.

For pictures of people or animals in low light conditions it is beneficial to have a red-eye reduction mode operating. This is possible with the SB26 and the in-built speedlight. The symbols to show that red-eye reduction is in operation are an eye symbol and a lightning bolt. They are displayed on the top-plate L.C.D..

When the flash has charged and we press fully down on the release a lamp lights for around a second before the actual picture taking flash fires.

For special needs or to be adventurous try the following techniques:-

Rear Curtain TTL Flash

In the normal synchronisation mode the flash fires as soon as an exposure starts. The shutter is made up of two separate curtains and it is upon the following principle that exposure is based.

1) The shutter release button is depressed.

2) Milliseconds later a command signal starts the first shutter travelling from the top to the bottom of the shutter gate or frame. The flash fires at the same time.

3) The second curtain starts to travel at a delay that varies from almost instantaneously after the first curtain or many seconds later, depending upon the camera in use and the synchronisation speed used.

4) The TTL flash control quenches the output from the speedlight.

5) Both the first and second curtains close with a delay between them dependent upon the above.

With REAR curtain synchronisation the flash illumination is fired just as the second curtain travels, so the exposure has already recorded much of the image with existing light.

Q. What are the advantages of REAR curtain TTL flash?

A. For many people there are now real benefits of using this technique. The type of image that gains from this is one that has an exposure that is quite lengthy, say one second and a moving subject in the picture. There is really no point in using REAR curtain TTL for fast synchronisation speeds as the shutter opens and closes so quickly that the effect, if there is any movement, is not seen. REAR curtain synchronisation is indicated by the lightning bolt symbol and the word REAR shown together. Please note that when using an SB25 or SB26 the setting for REAR curtain synchronisation is made on the speedlight, NOT on the F70/N70.

Slow Synchronisation Flash

This is an altogether more useful technique. With this mode the shutter speed fires at a slower speed than normal. This has the effect of allowing more light onto the film that is not flash but existing light. After the brief flash has fired this is still recording on film. The areas of the image where this will be noticed are those that are outside of the flash range. We can therefore, by using Slow Synchronisation, render more detail in outside portraits in low light, interior shots will record a beautiful glow from lamps etc. and the background. When we use either the Night scene or Motion Effect Programs from the Vari-Program menus, Slow Sync flash is activated if we use a speedlight.

Q. Can I combine REAR curtain TTL flash and Slow Sync flash?

A. Yes we can. But not together on the top-plate display. Set REAR on the camera and use Shutter-Priority to set our desired slow synchronisation speed.

Slow synchronisation does have one drawback - holding the camera steady if no support is used. The effects of camera shake can be masked by the brief flash which freezes the action at that time, but different people and lens combinations can suffer to greater or lesser degrees. Slow synchronisation is indicated by the lightning bolt and the word SLOW next to it.

The F70/N70 indicates to us when it recommends the use of flash by illuminating a lightning bolt symbol in yellow. We can of course ignore this but don't be afraid to take comparative shots with and without flash using the above modes at our disposal.

Setting The F70/N70 For TTL Flash Control:

1) Pressure should be taken on the FUNCTION button and the Command Input Dial turned until the pointer is inside the flash mode box.

2) Release pressure from the Command Input Dial and place it on the SET button. Turn the Command Input Dial until the flash symbol we want is on display

N.B. If using an SB24, SB25 or SB26 we should set REAR curtain synchronisation on the camera and not on the Speedlight.

Q. Can I use any film speed for TTL flash control?

A. No. The recommended film speeds are between 25 and 1000 I.S.O.. Most people do not realise that this is the widest range of speeds with which any camera can operate and guarantee correct exposure in most situations. As an example consider that the FE2 camera which, although discontinued by Nikon some years ago, is still a favourite of many, but only had a TTL range of 25/400 I.S.O.. The F70/N70 surely copes with most of the films we are likely to use, but again don't be afraid to experiment with film speeds slower or faster. Indeed I know many press photographers who will, when appropriate, use TTL flash control with films in excess of 1000 I.S.O..

The TTL control of flash is designed to work with two styles once we have chosen from the control methods mentioned above. These are Standard TTL and Balanced TTL.

Standard TTL Flash Control

Think of this as the traditional method of flash control, where the basic premise is that the flash will fire and the exposure be based on this illumination alone. No account is taken, to all intents and purposes, of existing light such as daylight or man made illumination. Interior photographs are ideally suited by this method. It requires the flash to often be quite strong and sometimes a flash must fire at its maximum output. If this happens the lightning bolt inside the viewfinder that glowed a steady red to indicate that the flash had fired will now pulsate. Under-exposure may have occurred if the full kick of the gun still was not enough. It is worth taking the shot again if possible moving closer to the subject or choosing a wider "F" stop setting. This mode operates automatically when the camera decides that the output required is too much for the other style of operation - Balanced Fill Flash or Fill Flash.

Balanced Fill Flash And Fill Flash

Balanced with what? What does it fill in? The answer to the first question is existing light - daylight or any other continuous source such as room lighting. The second answer applies to the darker areas of the composition that the flash illumination reaches, specifically the shadows.

If we were to fire Standard TTL flash in daylight, as an example for a portrait, the camera and flashgun work on the presumption that it is just the flash illumination that is lighting the image. As daylight in this example exists and in some strength, it too adds its effect to the image - over-exposure results!

The technique of balancing flash illumination with daylight is something that can be done by guess work, arithmetic and experience. It is no bad thing to experiment anyway as we should all develop a personal style. But in honesty it is more often than not better to use an automatic system for simplicity. Nikon have done a lot of good work on our behalf with the F70/N70.

Q. Why use flash with daylight - what are the benefits?

A. When we look at a scene our eyes adjust to the differing levels of brightness, particularly in very bright light. Film relies on its recording range or exposure latitude to capture this range of brightness levels. Unfortunately no film can capture entirely the range of brightness that we see comfortably with our eyes. By using Fill Flash we introduce extra light into the scene. As it is weaker than the brighter areas of the image it has no effect on them. The darker areas or shadows are however "lifted" or filled in, to reveal more detail in them and reducing the range of contrast the film now has to record, making the image look more in tune to the one we saw; although don't expect a 100% match.

When we use one of the Matrix metering systems, the term used to describe the effect (with built-in or add-on TTL speedlight) is Balanced Fill Flash, rather than Fill Flash. Matrix metering sets an exposure for the background made with existing light, while the TTL flash system is used to fill in the shadows and other low light areas to give a similar or balanced effect. If we use the Spot or Centre-Weighted metering options a fill in flash is still achieved, but the daylight exposure for the background is not automatically set to record in a similar vain. If it does, then this is down to a little bit of luck or precise metering on our part so the actual "F" stop and shutter speed set with these metering methods matches the combinations needed for a correct exposure of the background anyway.

Synchronisation Speed

When we are in either one of the programmed options or Aperture-Priority, the F70/N70 selects its own sync speed. With the normal flash mode, with or without red-eye reduction, the speed selected will vary between a 1/60th of a second and a 1/125th of a second depending on how the camera accesses the situation. When REAR or Slow curtain synchronisation is used, the shutter speed can go as long as 30 seconds!

With Shutter-Priority or Manual exposure in operation, we set the speed at which the flash is to be synchronised, with the limitations already noted.

Even More Special Flash Controls .....

TTL Flash Compensation

We may find that we often obtain images that are a little too strong or weak for our personal tastes and characteristics of film and lab. If this is the case then this is a feature for you. In effect it will tone down or increase the flash output in 1/3rd E.V. steps away from its normal amount from -3 E.V. less, up to a maximum of 1 E.V. more. I have found in the past that most Japanese flash systems give a little too much light for Balanced Fill Flash for my liking. Therefore I have tended to set this feature to -2/3rd E.V. when photographing Caucasian skin. Once again however do not be afraid to experiment as the stronger effect has its place as well for more dramatic, surreal and creative portraits.

Setting TTL Flash Compensation:

1) Hold the FUNCTION button down and turn the Command Input Dial until the pointer is inside the box to the left of the Flash mode controls already mentioned. A '+/-' next to a lightning bolt appears. The latter is against a black background.

2) Release pressure and press down onto the SET button. While doing this turn the Command Input Dial until the desired amount of compensation is set. The amount of

compensation is indicated inside the semi circle in place of the frame count until we remove pressure from the SET button.

Once this feature is activated it remains so whenever we use the in-built speedlight or a TTL dedicated flash. Inside the viewfinder the same lightning bolt and the '+/-' are displayed on the right of the L.C.D. panel.

TTL Flash Exposure Bracketing

This feature is ideal to use to determine the amount of compensation you will prefer, or as an excellent way to produce a variety of shots of the same subject but with different amounts of flash. The way the system works is to provide a range of shots, each of which has a different amount of flash used. The amount of flash can vary between .3 E.V., .5 E.V., .7 E.V. and 1 E.V. A word of advice. If you are using colour print or negative film I would suggest that you start your experiments at .7 or 1 E.V.. With transparency emulsions .3 or .5 E.V. are more suitable with regard to the film's characteristics.

In all circumstances the F70/N70 will take 3 shots in the bracketing sequence. The first will be under exposed by the amount we set, the second will be the normal flash exposure as the camera sees it, while the third will be over exposed by the amount we set. The bar graph that appeared in the Manual Exposure mode will show to indicate that the sequence is operating and adjusting the exposure.

Setting TTL Flash Exposure Bracketing:

1) Bring the built-in speedlight to its active position or switch the speedlight in the hot-shoe on.

2) The box on the left side of the green panel is the one in which TTL flash exposure bracketing appears. A lightning bolt and the letters BKT are displayed in the box and blink

when the pointer is in this box. Use the FUNCTION button and Command Dial to select it.

3) The amount of compensation we set is shown in the semi circle instead of the frame count. Take three shots by pressing the shutter release button each time. This is required even if CH or CL advance modes are active. The amount that each shot is compensated by is displayed as we take each shot. At the end of the three shots the sequence is cancelled and the frame count returns.

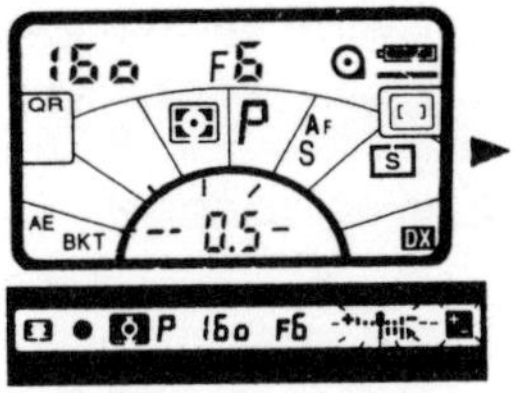

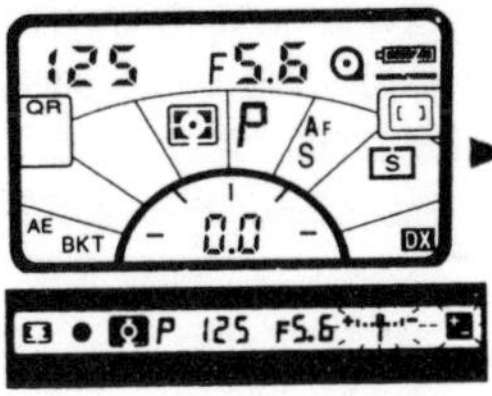

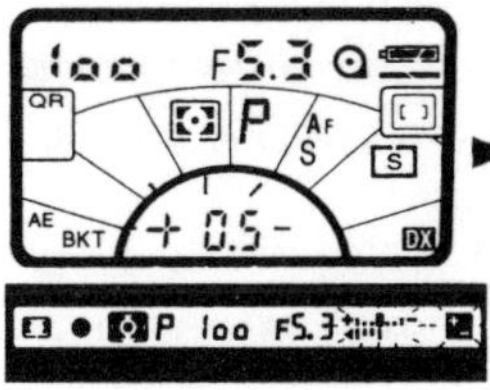

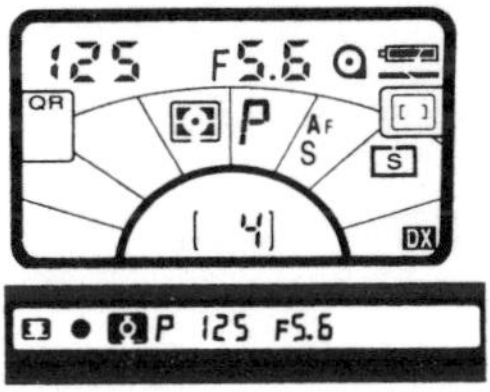

The TTL compensation and the bracketing sequence work with any Nikon TTL speedlight and many independent guns dedicated to Nikon. I must add that Nikon quite rightly cannot guarantee any other make of unit as some may damage the F70/N70. This would tend to be, however, with older units. The final choice must be left to you.

Q. I want to use a speedlight off of the hot-shoe and retain dedication, how do I do it?

A. The SC17 is the TTL lead you require to take a normal hot-shoe flash away from the camera and maintain TTL dedication. It is coiled but when uncoiled it is 1.5m long. More than one can be attached together (but it's not cheap).

Q. I want to use two TTL speedlights together how can I do this?

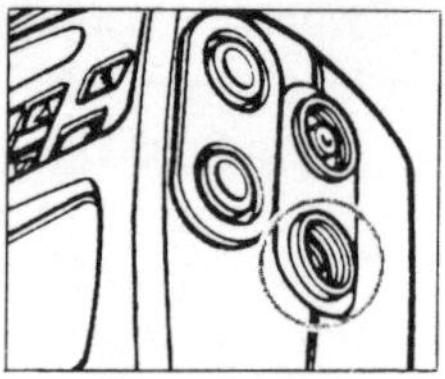

SB26 Sockets

A. If we want both units off camera then an SC17 is the first lead we need. At the end, where the first flash unit sits, there are also two terminals that are the connection points for other leads. Into one or both of these we can fit an SC18 (1.5m) or SC19 (3m) TTL lead. They run directly into similar sockets on a SB24, SB25 or SB26. Other units without these sockets will fit into an AS10 which does have the appropriate sockets. The newest professional speedlight is the SB26. This has a built-in slave unit which triggers the SB26 when it senses another flash firing. It has a special delay mode that Nikon claim will enable TTL flash to operate on another gun. Leadless TTL flash - nice one!

Q. I want TTL dedication but don't want the speedlight dangling on the SC17 without a support. What can I do?

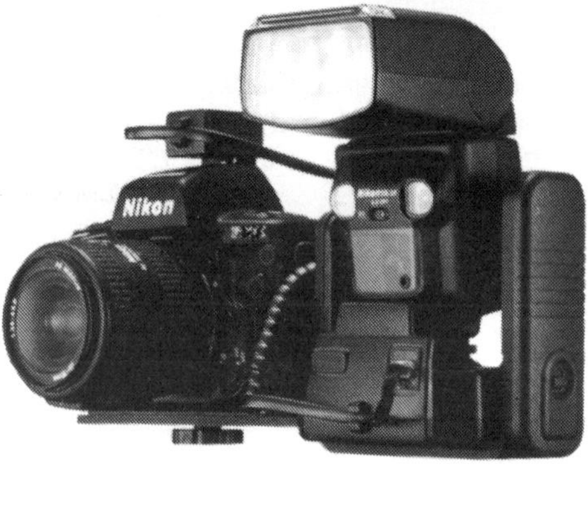

Nikon Power Bracket Unit SK-6

A. Nikon make a unit called a SK6. It is a pretty unique approach to a flash bracket. It has its own built-in connecting lead so an SC17 is not required. There are also batteries housed in the base of the SK6 which speed up the recharge time as they work with the batteries in the speedlight.

More About Flash Photography With The F70/N70

If we intend to use AF with flash it should be noted that we cannot use Wide Area AF. Spot AF is the only option available. This is due to two reasons. The first is because of a red beam omitted from the front of many speedlights in low light. This is called the AF assist beam and it helps the focus system by producing a patterning on a subject for the focus to lock onto. The beam roughly corresponds to the area of Spot AF. The second reason is the way that electronic detection works - there could be problems with exposure and finding focus with Wide Area AF. Like it or not, the F70/N70 automatically makes Spot AF operative when we have set Wide AF and have activated a speedlight. When we use the SK6, the AF assistance beam does not operate at all. Again there is a problem. The off-camera position of the flash means that it would not cover the area that the AF sensor looks at. The very first SK6 units I saw did have the beam operative but this has since been changed as the beam has absolutely no effect when the SK6 is used.

There is a chance that the built-in speedlight like any gun will get hot if used rapidly and repeatedly. The instruction manual states that it should be rested after firing it for 20 consecutive times with less than 5 seconds between each shot. A 10 minute rest is recommended (no, the flash not the photographer)!

Q. My F70/N70 will not trigger an independently made flash unit that I have used for many years previously - why?

A. This is a classic example of the camera telling us something is wrong. Sometimes we obtain one flash and then no more. This is because the electrical current is too high for the camera. I would recommend that the unit is not used again with the F70/N70. Switch off and disconnect it. Now, switch the camera on and this should reset the F70/N70 to be able to accept another flash unit.

If the exposure bar graph similar to the one that shows in Manual exposure mode appears in Aperture-Priority or Shutter-Priority, it is informing us that the background will be over- or under-exposed by the amount shown when compared to the TTL flash exposure. If we adjust the camera's controls we can correct for this or we can of course leave things as they are depending on our artistic impressions.

Chapter Six
Customising The F70/N70 - Choosing Accessories

How do we adapt the basic body for our needs? The first thing to mention is that you will not need each and every accessory Nikon and independent companies produce. A photographer buys and uses only what he or she needs. There are always, however, those items that are a photographic must. Let us start with something as important as, or possibly more important than, the camera - the lens.

Nikkor lenses are renowned around the world for their high resolution, contrast and aberration correction properties. The current range of AFD Nikkor lenses continues to grow. No matter. For our needs and tastes there is a range of optics available from Nikon alone that far outweighs our requirements. Here are a few comments about each to help those who are new to the system.

Fisheye and Wide Angle Optics

This is a series of lenses where we are becoming spoilt for choice. Having said that there is a great difference between wide angle lenses as far as the amount of a subject/scene they record, even when talking about a few millimetres difference. More so than say on telephoto type lenses. I strongly recommend that the correct lens hood is used. This will help avoid flare reducing the image quality. The series starts with a 16mm fisheye lens with a 180° angle of view and runs to the 35mm lens with a 62° angle (taken from the diagonal of the format).

AFD Nikkor 16mm f2.8

This is the widest angle lens in the AF series having a 180° angle of view. It is an amazing lens when used in the right circumstances. It has a visual impact that gives an amazing spatial depth to the image. Characteristically called a fisheye lens as its shape of the front element resembles just that. It is not corrected for bowing straight lines at the edge of the image so a wall, for instance, will look very strange indeed if it is positioned at the edge of the frame. Objects in the centre have a more natural appearance. I like this lens for occasional images but it is not one, as far as I am aware, that photographers use as a regular lens.

AFD Nikkor 18mm f2.8

Another very wide lens with a 100° angle of view but not a fisheye. As this is the fastest 18mm lens Nikon have ever produced its front element is large and takes 77mm filters that can be expensive. The lens has to be thought about to justify its price and I must say that in use I have not seen a different image quality from the lower priced 20mm lens. The angle of view and the "F" stop are the reasons for purchasing this lens. Dramatic landscapes are possible but due to the large area of a scene recorded be careful that shooting against the sky does not cause lens flare. Do not forget that for work in confined areas the SB26 now covers the 18mm lens coverage!

AFD Nikkor 20mm f2.8

I like this lens. An angle of view of 94° that gives a great opportunity for pictures in small spaces, a good landscape lens and, I feel, good value for money. It has 62mm attachments like many of the other Nikkor lenses. The SB25 and SB26 both cover this with their flash angle.

AFD Nikkor 24mm f2.8

For some time now this has been the wide angle lens that I have used the most. I think it is a very good lens indeed. For those who want to travel it does not take up much space. A lens that can be used for all but the most critical copy and architectural work due to its correction properties. Do not let

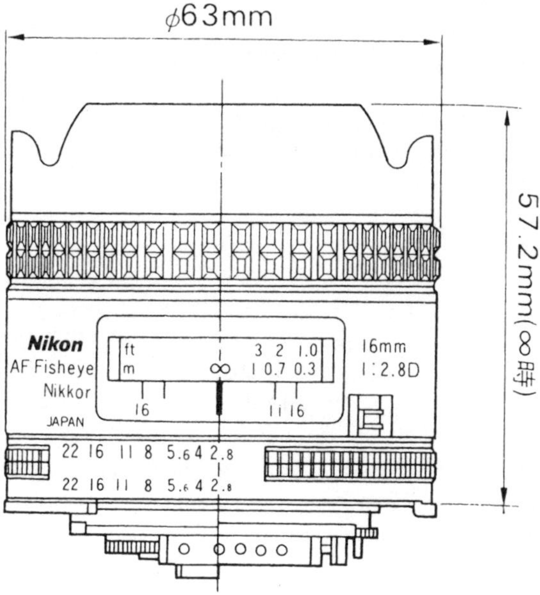

AF Fisheye 16mm f2.8 "D" Lens

me put you off with that last comment as this would be my wide angle to take to a desert island. It has a 84° coverage and a 52mm attachment size, making it very useful for those of us who use filters sparingly but when required on a different number of optics. The 52mm size is common to many wide angle and 50mm lenses.

AFD Nikkor 28mm f2.8

Once again a small and lightweight lens. It covers 74°. This is one of the recent additions to the "D" series so I have not yet used this lens that extensively. I find though that the angle of view is somehow not quite wide enough for much of my work.

AFD Nikkor 28mm f1.4

An amazing lens in terms of its speed - a world first. Due to its cost I won't dwell on it, but if your tastes are for low light work or night time photography, it is worth finding out more about it. The angle of view is 74° and it accepts 72mm filters.

AF Nikkor 35mm f2

So far not a lens updated to "D" type technology. What a lens! Many find the idea of it boring, but the quality is exceptional. I think this is Nikon's best ever 35mm lens and that says something bearing in mind the MF 35mm f2. As many zooms cover this focal length, or a 50mm lens is used instead, the sales of this lens are small, but I can honestly say I have never heard one complaint from anyone who has used it.

50mm Lenses

AF 50mm Nikkor f1.8

The smallest and lightest Nikkor AF lens. Its price, due to mass production, belies the fact that this is more than a competent performer. An excellent starting point with which to team the F70/N70. The angle of coverage is 46°.

AF 50mm Nikkor f1.4

Like the f1.8, this lens has still to become a "D" type. It shares the same angle of view. I have one of the early AF version that is incredible at the wider "F" stop settings. Heavier than its smaller brother, I have no qualms about its quality but for many my advice is still, the f1.8 unless you must have the extra speed.

Telephoto Lenses

AFD Micro 60mm Nikkor f2.8

If the budget will stretch to it and the extra weight and size are not a problem this is a high quality and versatile optic for general use. Close-up images are razor sharp and the close focusing means that we can reproduce images that are life size on film. 62mm attachment filters are required. The angle of view is 39°.

AFD 85mm f1.8

If I did not already own a 85mm f2 MF lens, this would be on my list. Quick AF speed, exceptional optical characteristics for portraits - what more can I say. Oh! It has a 28° angle of view and takes 62mm attachments. A lens hood is supplied with this lens.

AFD 105mm Micro Nikkor f2.8

Having already commented about this lens briefly in the text all I would add is - get one if you can. It may need a little softening for portraits as it is that sharp. An angle of view of 23° and a 52mm attachment size, it shares the same magnification as the 60mm, but at a greater lens to subject distance. This is useful in close-up work in order to light the subject with flash.

AFD 105mm Nikkor f2 DC

As a straight portrait lens this is ideal in both terms of focal length, "F" stop speed and image quality. I am not so sure that the defocus facility (hence the term DC) is as good as is claimed but I would use it without this feature if I did not already have a 105mm Micro Nikkor. A 72mm attachment size is not unduly large bearing in mind the "F" stop. The angle of view is 23° and the lens is made with a hood already fitted.

AFD 105mm Nikkor f2DC

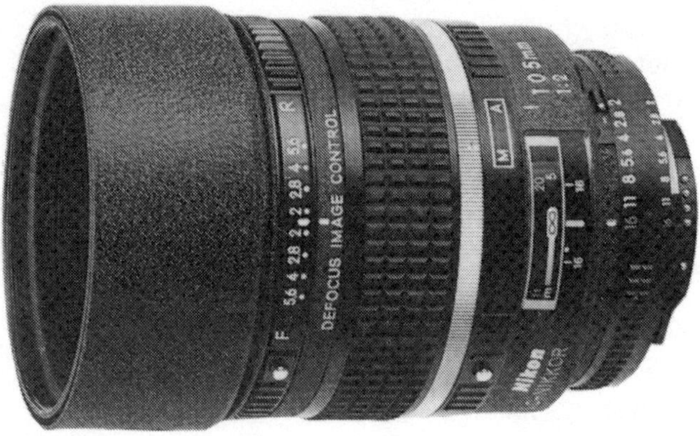

AF 135mm Nikkor f2 DC

The comments I have made for the 105mm Defocus lens are applicable to this lens. The 135mm focal length is not as common as it once was and I wonder if Nikon regret the production of this lens, preferring to produce just the 105? Do not let me put you off though, as once again, you cannot go wrong with its portrait characteristics. The same filter size as the 105mm lens, but with an angle of view of 18°. The hood is built on.

AFD 180mm Nikkor f2.8

This lens will be available shortly after this book first goes on sale. It will, to the best of my knowledge, be of the same optical performance as the 180mm AF currently available. Why change something that works? I cannot speak too highly once again about its performance, but seriously consider whether the focal length is applicable to your work. A 72mm filter size is included on the lens as is an integral lens hood and case. The angle of view is 13°.

AF 300mm Nikkor f4

Another lens out of the top draw! Don't be put off by anyone who rates the faster f2.8 lens of this focal length as the superior lens - this lens is *that* good. Well made with a tripod bush fitted as is the lens hood. The angle of view is around 8°. The lens accepts front fitting filters but more usually filters that slip into its turret of 39mm size.

AFI 300mm Nikkor f2.8 (Distance Technology)

Wow! - Not just the price. A sports photographer's standard lens in many ways. Tripod bush, lens hoods and front cover are supplied in one of those aluminium cases with the name NIKON stamped on its outside. The in-built motor makes the AF very, very fast and quiet. The angle of view is approximately 8° and the lens takes 39mm filters not at the front but in the turret of the lens.

AFI 400mm Nikkor f2.8 (Distance Technology)

Ouch! - Not just the price, but the weight of this optical beast. The same comments apply as for the 300mm AFI.

AFI 500mm Nikkor f4 (Distance Technology)

Again this is a relatively new lens, which sadly I have only had a little time to try out. If it is as good as the MF 500mm F4P, then Nikon have no worries. Relatively lightweight, many nature photographers use this lens a lot. Hood, aluminium case and tripod bush are supplied. This lens accepts filters again inside its turret of a 39mm size. The angle of view is 5°.

AFI 600mm Nikkor f4 (Distance Technology)

At 6,050 grams this is a heavy lens. It has a narrow angle of view of approximately 4°. It is supplied with the same attachments and accessories as the AFI lenses.

Zoom Lenses

AFD 20/35mm Zoom Nikkor f2.8

Many photographers involved in sports and photojournalism are still tying to get hold of one of these. Short supply has been caused by excessive demand. For most people the quality is every bit as good as their prime lenses. The 77mm filter size is large, but quality first! The angle of view ranges from 94 - 62°.

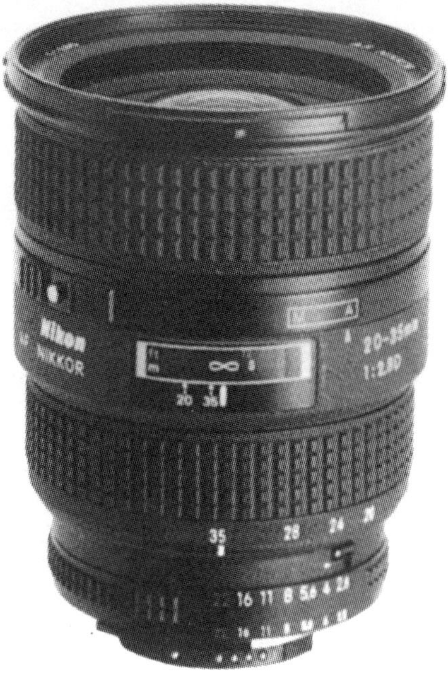

AFD 20/35mm Zoom Nikkor f2.8

AF 24/50mm Nikkor f3.3/4.5

A nice range of focal lengths. This lens is a good performer although I find the focusing ring a little loose for my liking. The filter size is 62mm and the angle of view is between 84 - 46°. This is a non "D" technology lens.

AFD 28/70mm Nikkor f3.5/4.5

The first Nikkor lens to be mass produced using an aspherical lens element. Small, light and good quality, it makes a perfect travel companion to the F70/N70 where a general purpose lens is required. 52mm attachments are accepted and the angle of view is between 74 - 34°.

AF 28/85mm Nikkor f3.5/4.5

I have always had difficulty appreciating this lens. It does cover a useful range! The angle of view is approximately 74 - 28° and it accepts 62m filters.

AFD 35/70mm Nikkor f2.8

One of the pro's favourites. 62mm filters and an angle of view between 62 - 34°. Quality in excess of most needs!

AFD 35/80m Nikkor f4/5.6

Not the best lens in the range but having used it for snap shots quite often, it is more than good enough for this type of application. For many it will be the first lens they use on the F70/N70 and it again makes a nice travel companion. Angle of view is between 62 - 30° and the lens accepts 52mm attachments.

AFD 35/105mm Nikkor f3.5/4.5

Another lens to be introduced shortly. The angle of view is approximately 62 - 23°. I like the focal length very much and intend to add one of these to my system sooner rather than later. It takes 52mm filters.

AF 35/135mm Nikkor f3.5/4.5

A rather large lens that has never made me say 'wow' when looking at the results. A very useful range of focal lengths though. 62mm filters are required.

AFD 70/210mm Nikkor f4/5.6

A popular range of focal lengths is covered with this lens. Light and more than capable for most people's needs. It takes 62mm filters and is supplied with a case.

AF 75/300mm Nikkor f4.5/5.6

The angle of coverage is around 31 - 40°. It stretches into the telephoto enough to require a small tripod bush being supplied with it. 62mm filters are attached when required. It is supplied with a case.

AFD 80/200mm Nikkor f2.8

What more can people say about this lens? It is simply the finest telephoto zoom Nikon have ever made. 77mm filters are required. A case is supplied. The angle of view is around 30 - 12°. Start saving but do consider the weight - 1,300 grams.

Q. Which of the manual focus Nikkor lenses currently available can I use?

A. All can be used with the F70/N70 but we lose all Programmed modes, Shutter-Priority, "F" stop indications and both forms of Matrix metering.

Some of the MF lenses have not been duplicated in AF or AFD types. The shift lenses spring immediately to mind as do the reflex Nikkor lenses. Do not discount the MF lenses as they still offer most of the very useful features. Just make sure that the MF lens you are intending to fit is of either the AI or AIS mounting type. If in doubt contact your Nikon distributor. On the front of those expensive lenses we can attach equally expensive (comparatively) Nikon filters. What I

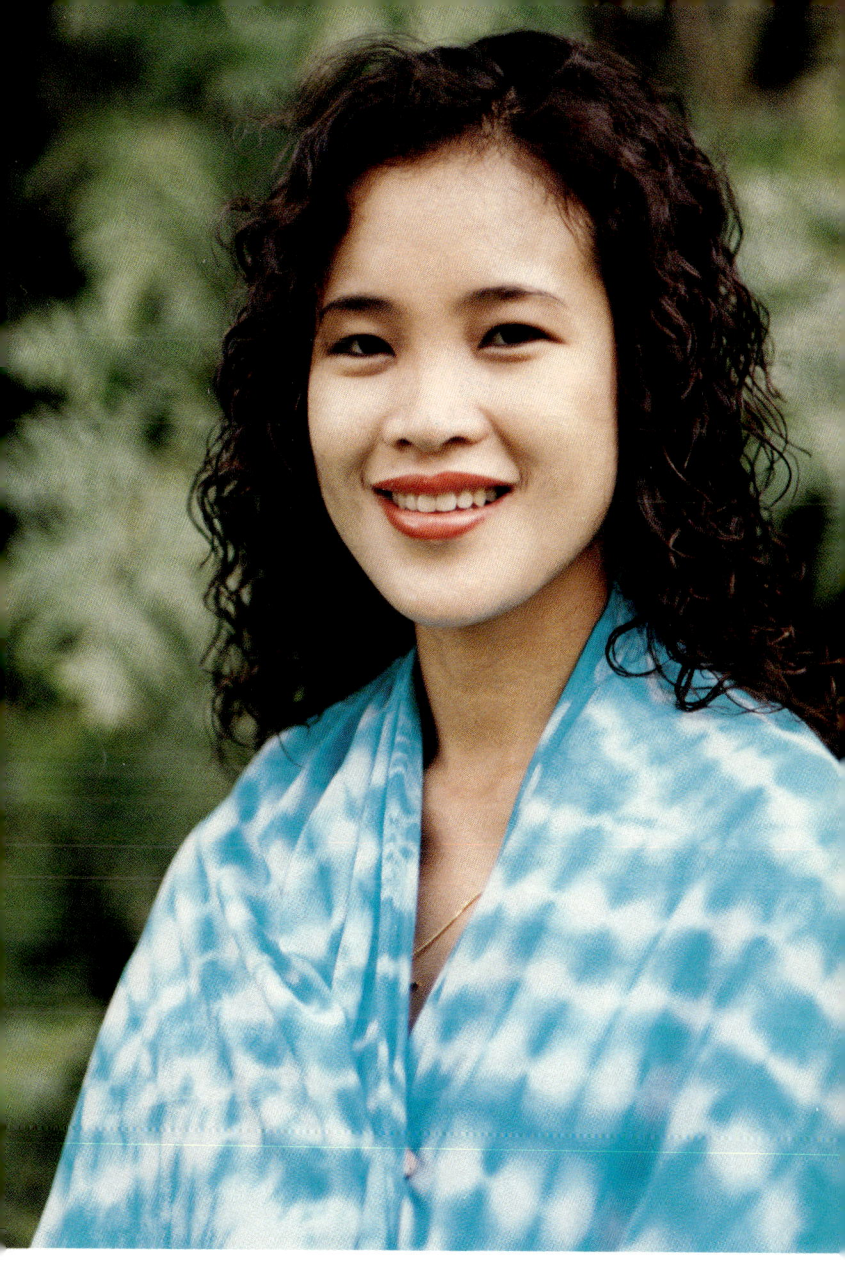

f2.8 aperture priority auto, lens
Nikon A/F 85mm f1.8D

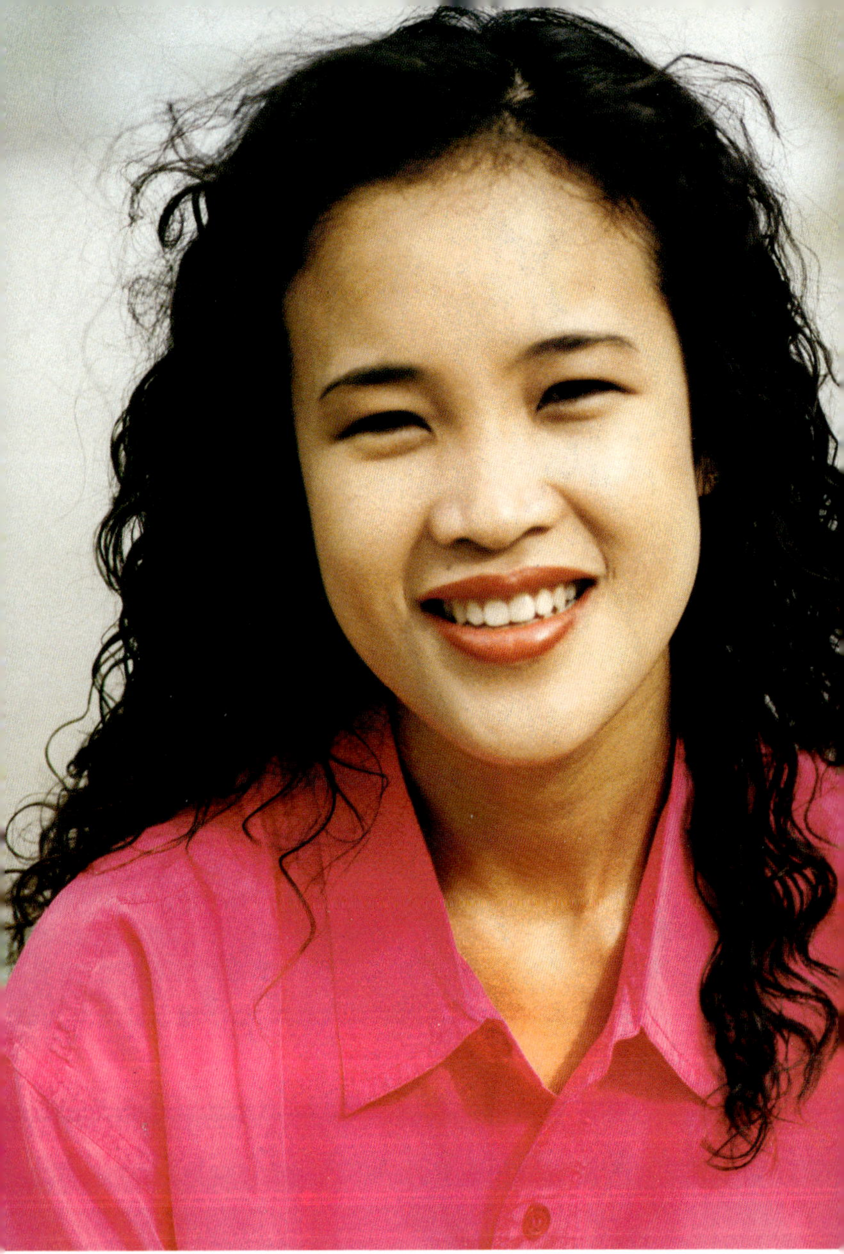

f2.8 again on aperture priority auto, lens
Nikon A/F 105mm f2 DCD

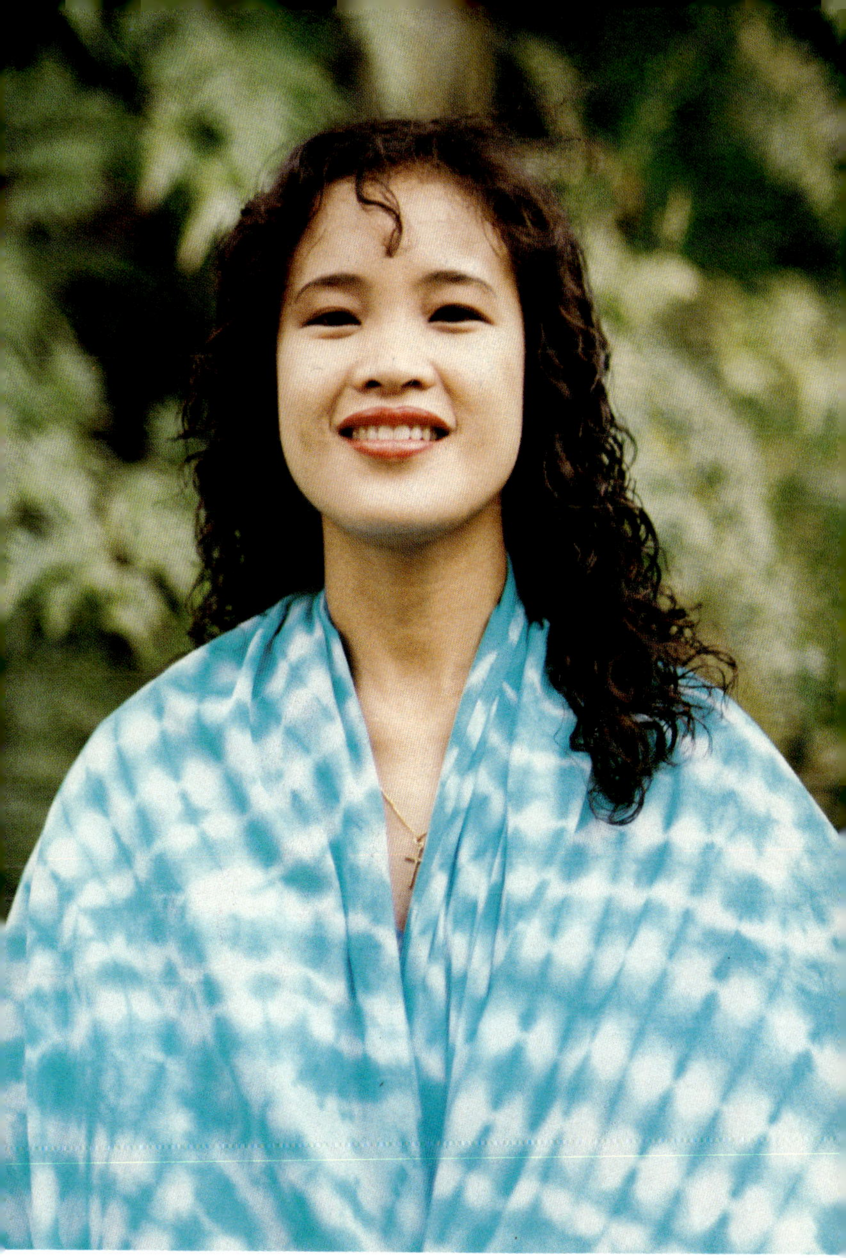

Standard Nikon A/F 50mm f1.8. Nikon F70/N70
set to programmed auto exposure control

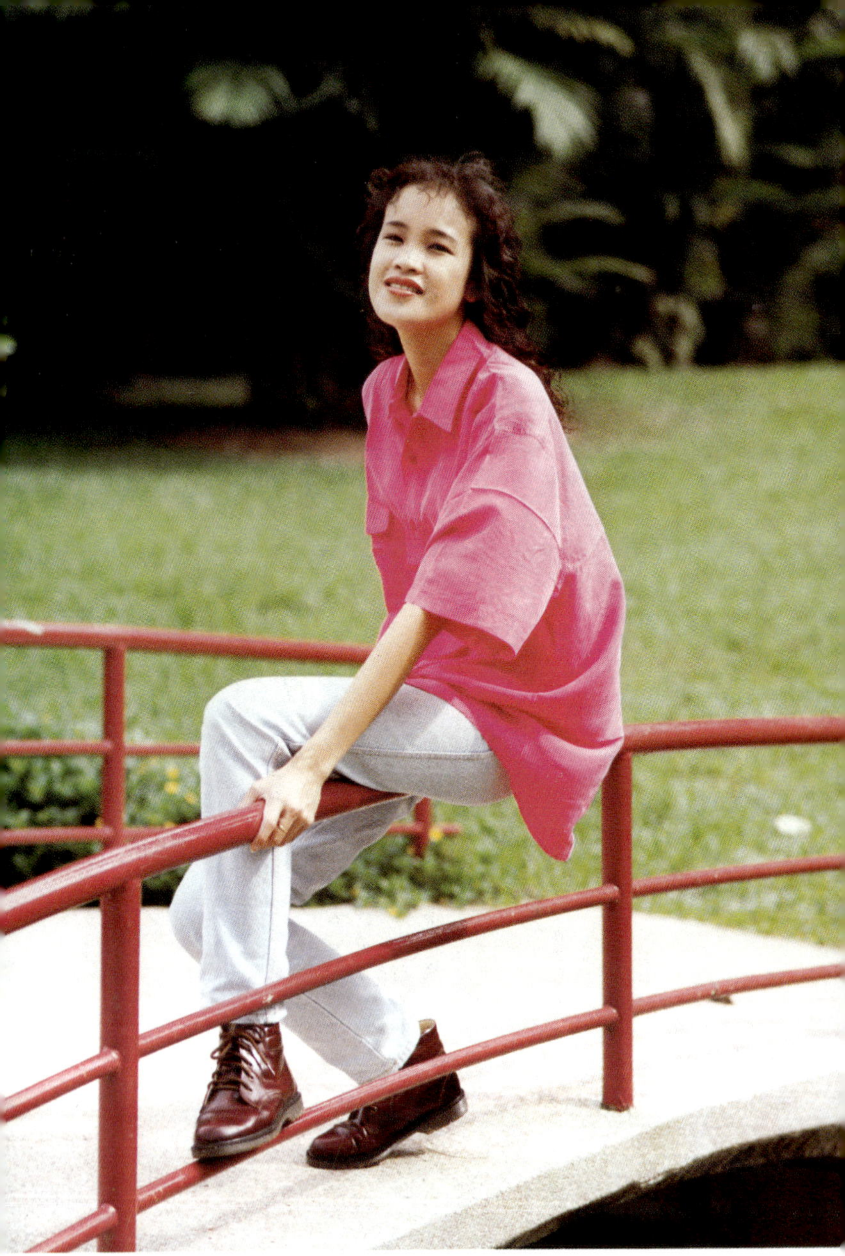

Nikon 35mm F2 A/F semi wide angle lens again on programmed auto exposure control

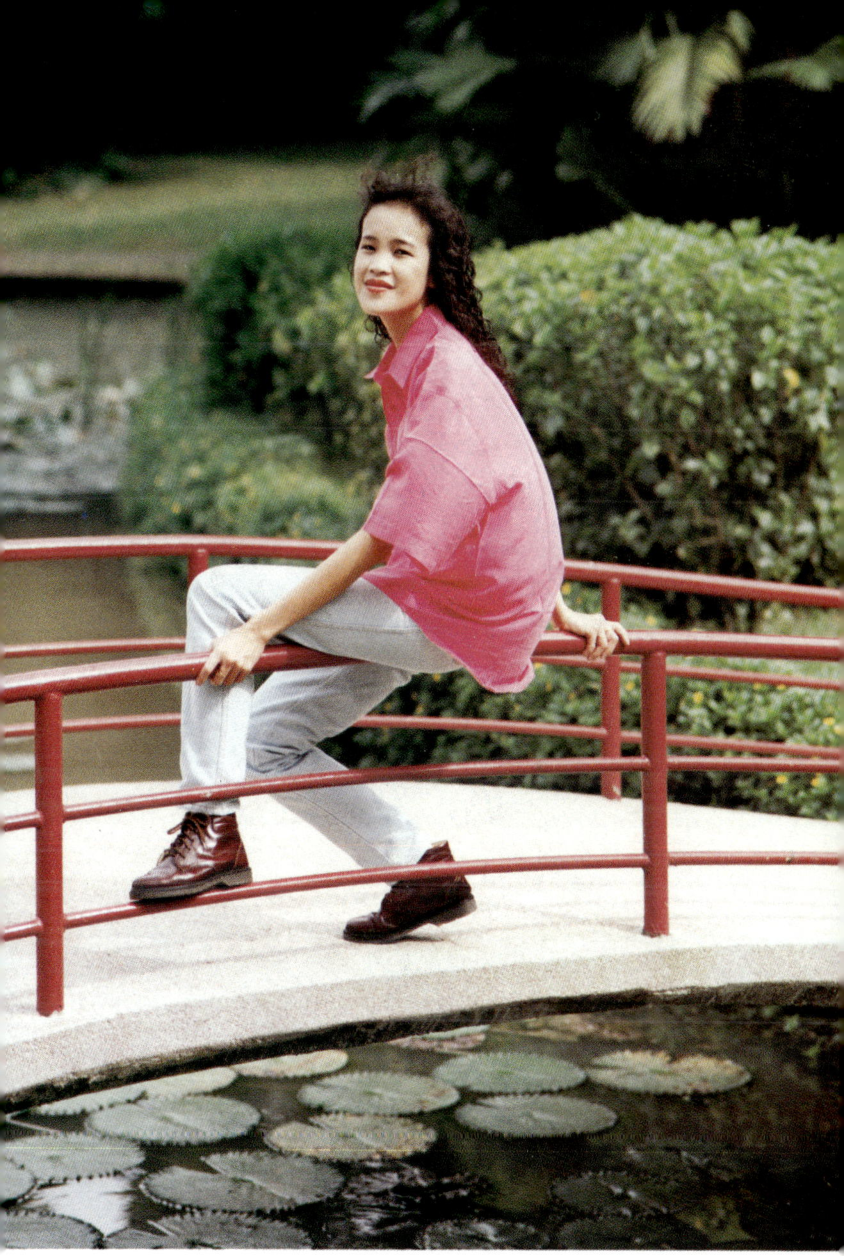

Perhaps the most usefull wide angle lens the 28mm.
It is important that you are not too close to your subject

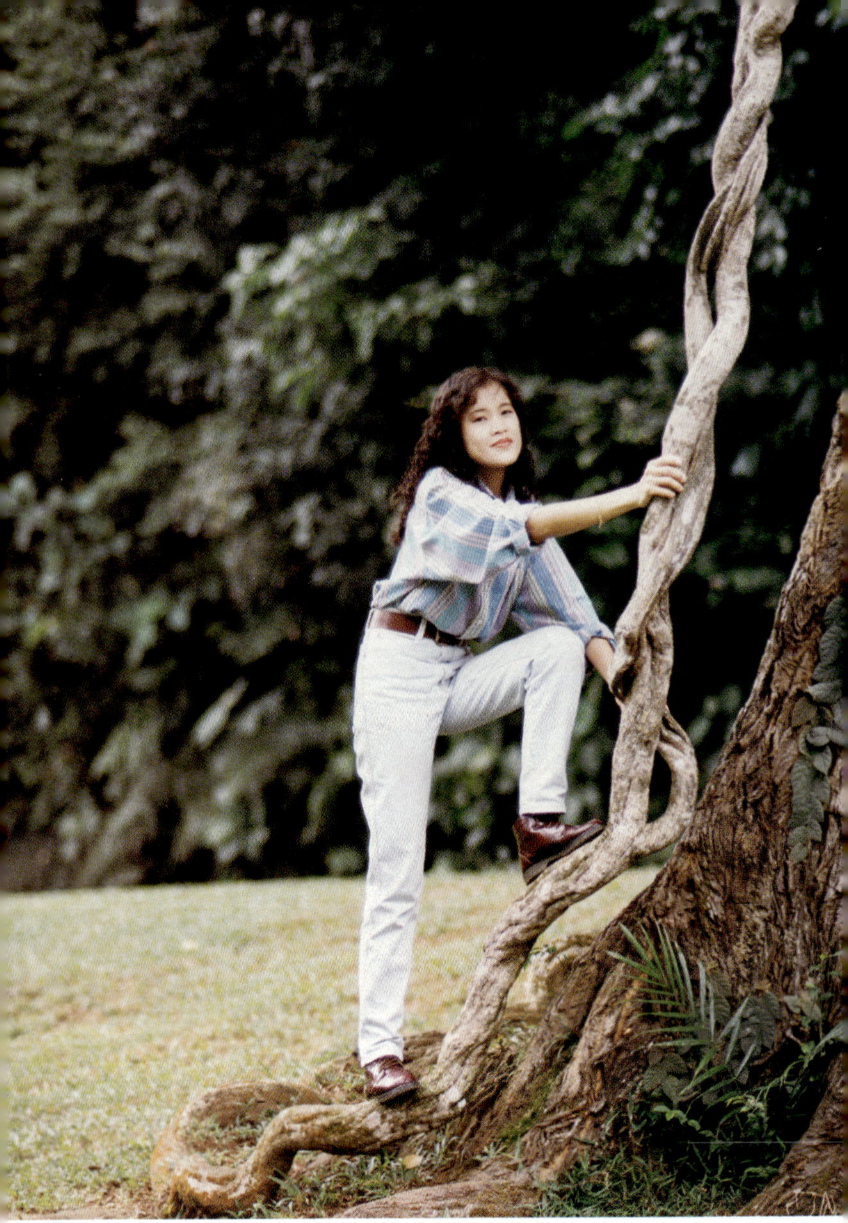

Lens Nikon 28 f2.8 A/F D. F70/N70
Set at manual exposure control for both aperture and shutter speed.

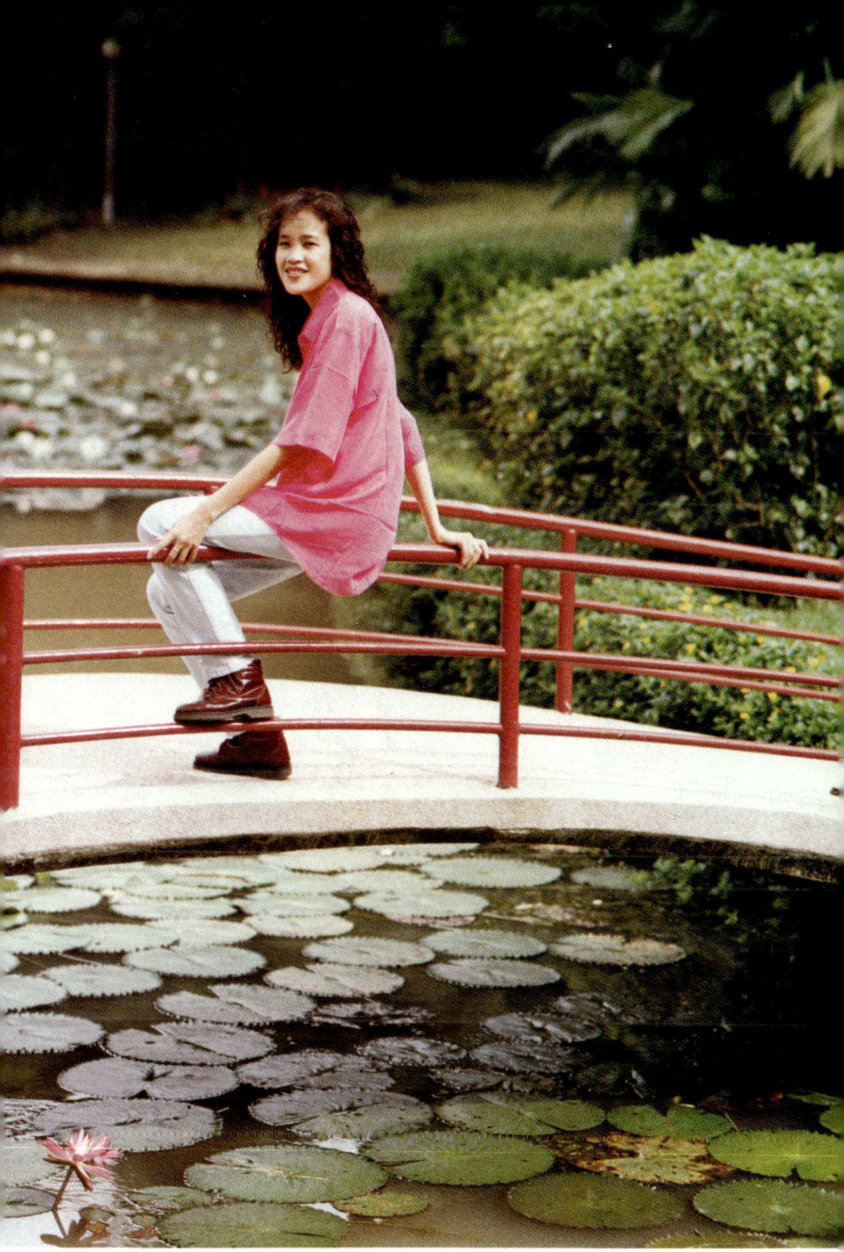

The F70/N70 with Nikon A/F 24mm f2.8D lens,
set on programmed auto exposure control

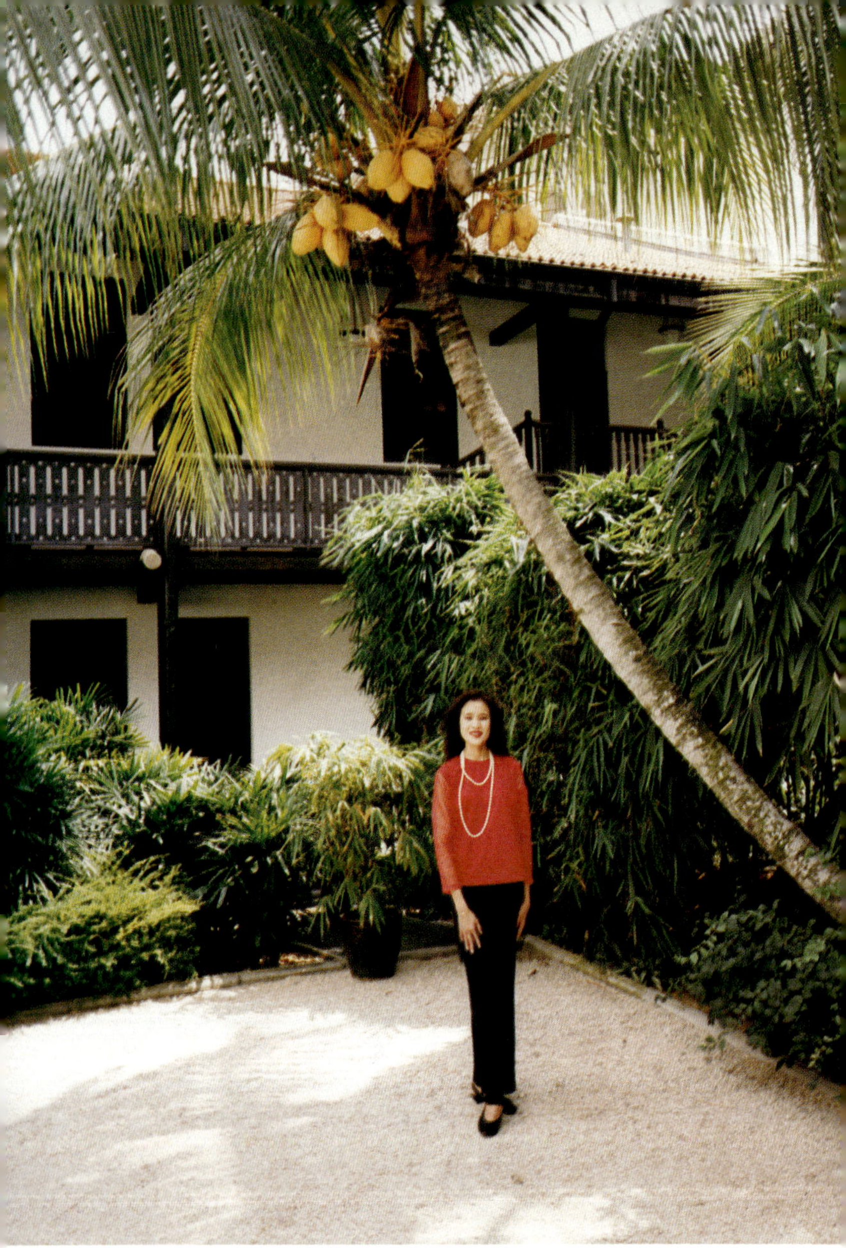

Your F70/N70 with 35 - 70 F2.8D
will enable you to frame your subject.

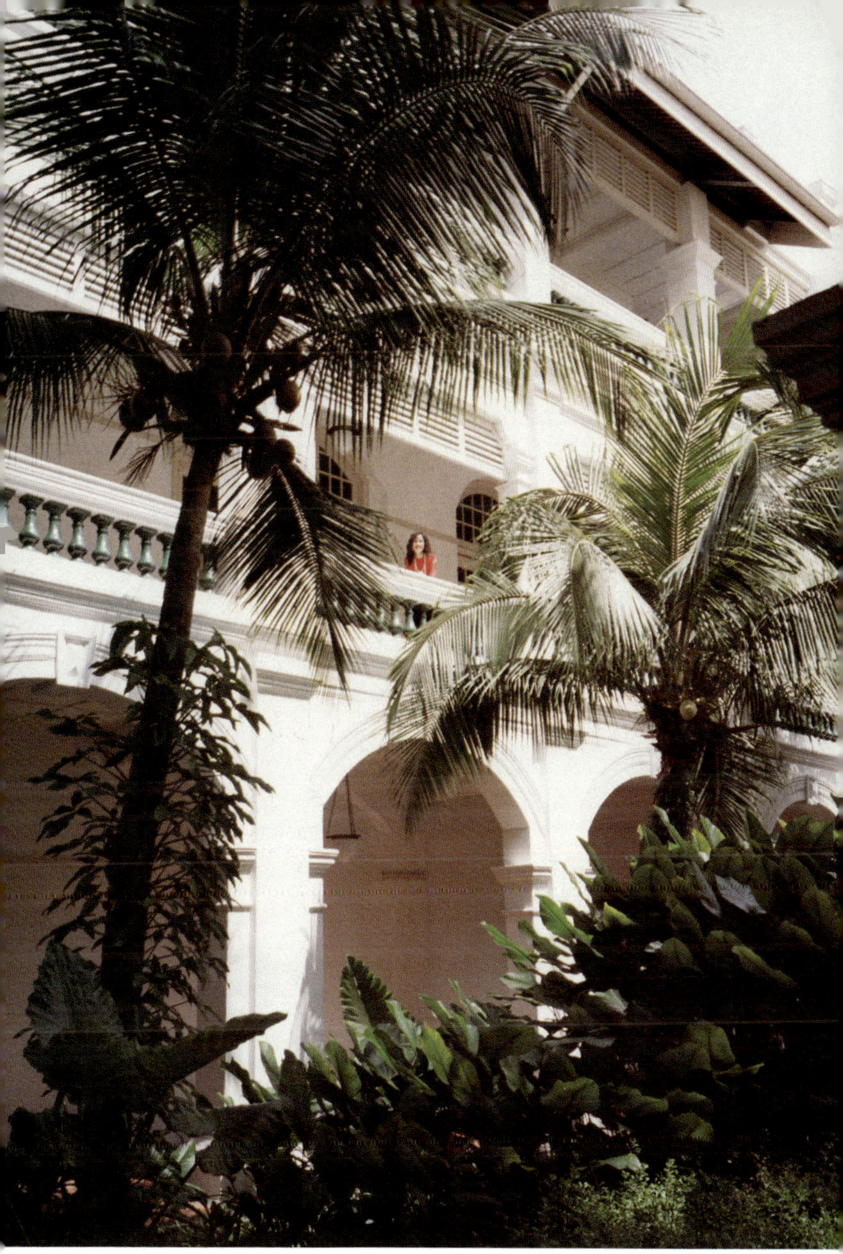

Nikon A/F 20mm f2.8D lens requires careful use to advoid converging verticals and distortion

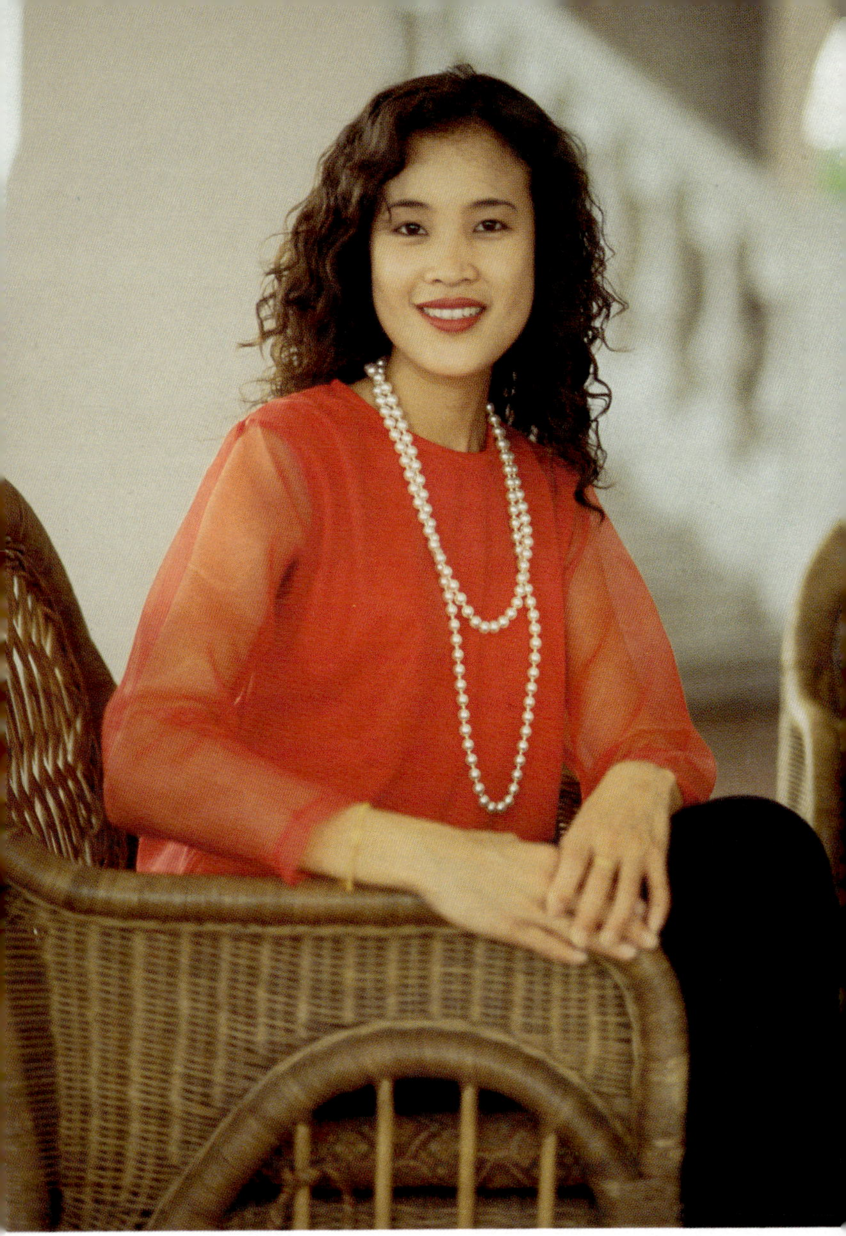

Try aperture priority, lens set to largest f. stop to put background out of focus. In this instance f. 3.5 on new AFD 35 / 105 mm zoom.

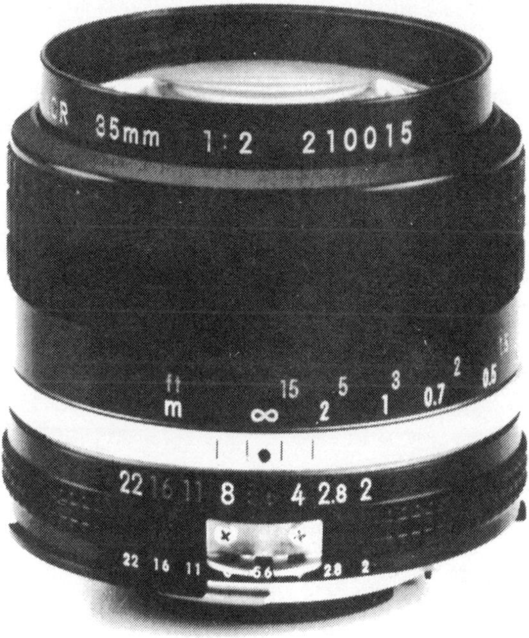

Nikkor Manual Focus Lens 35mm f2

would say in their defence is that they are made from the same glass, are mounted in thin rings to reduce the chance of vignetting and are superb optics.

Did you know that lenses suffer from vignetting, without any attachments? Vignetting is caused when the edges of a film do not receive as much light as the internal areas. This is a natural phenomenon, but can be aggravated by certain types of lens designs and attachments on the front of a lens.

Although this may be so small as to be irrelevant this is the case with all photographic lenses. To avoid this problem from exaggeration, if you can, use filters like the Nikon ones first or the excellent B+W alternatives made from Schott glass. I use both and can speak from many years experience. Vignetting can also be reduced by stopping a lens down around two stops from its widest setting.

So, what other accessories are there for the F70/N70? I would make sure that the image you see in the viewfinder is the best possible. This means considering diopter correction lenses and an eye cup as discussed in an earlier chapter.

There are a number of ways that an F70/N70 can be triggered remotely. First for most people would be the MC12A electronic cable release. This is 1.5m long and fits like all releases into the two pin socket on the front of the camera. The MC12A has a large plunger that enables a smooth triggering operation to be used. For BULB exposures there is also a lock to enable us to release pressure but keep the exposure operating.

For those who prefer or already have a traditional release the MR3 adapter enables this to be used. Nikons own cable release is called an AR3 and is around 30cm long? If you use an F90/N90 series camera and use the MC20 release for that, an adapter, MC25, will convert this for use on the F70/N70.

But for completely remote operation there are two other alternatives. The MW2 radio release set operates in good conditions up to 700m while in built-up areas it still has a very effective range of 150m, while the ML2 modulated light outfit triggers the F70/N70 from up to 100m away.

There are two cases available for the F70/N70. They are the CF51 and 52. In my experience I do not know one professional photographer who uses one, as the need is generally more than for just these two items. A good quality, well made and well known gadget bag is far more practical in my opinion.

For the close-up enthusiast there is a wealth of supporting items. Close-up attachment lenses screw into the front of a lens to enable it to focus much closer. Nikon currently make

7 types depending upon the lens we use and the magnification we desire. We can reverse lenses with the BR2a adapter which means that for the price of this small unit a high magnification is possible. There are many more close-up units that are available to make the job easier and more enjoyable.

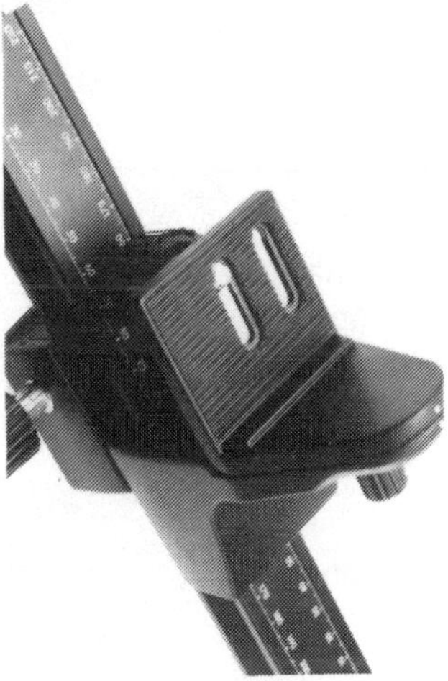

When tripod mounted, a camera attached to the PG2 slides backwards or forwards to find focus easily and without continually adjusting the tripod's position.

Now then, what about taking advantage of, for me, one of the F70/N70's endearing features - TTL flash control? At the time of writing Nikon produce 4 speedlights that offer TTL control and autofocus assistance in low light. They are the SB26, SB23, SB22 and SB20. I suspect that 90% of the sales Nikon will make for an F70/N70 will come from one of these or a future addition in the series. There are currently available an SB21B macro ring flash, SB16B, SB14 and SB11 speedlights still available that will give TTL compatibility, but no AF assistance. Of the discontinued speedlights the SB24 and SB25 are still in my opinion highly compatible and desirable, while a unit from yesteryear never fails to remind me what a super little unit it was - an SB15.

Now to highlight some of the interesting features of the SB26, the top of the line Speedlight, not already commented upon.

SB26 Speedlight

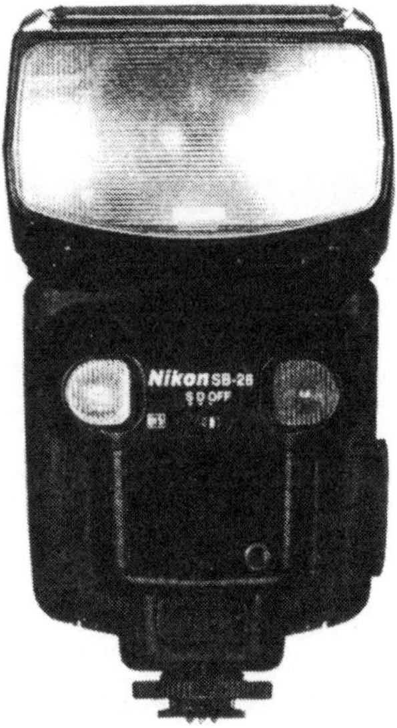

This unit is powerful. It has a guide number of 42m. Bounce and swivel are provided as are manual output level options from full power to 1/64th. Auto flash, over a very large range of "F" stops, only adds to its versatility with less capable cameras than the F70/N70.

But for us we will normally switch the SB26 to its TTL position. If we have set it, the speedlight will then use its computer controlled system to set the internal diffusers at a position to match as near as possible the focal length of lens on the camera. The range is from 24mm up to 85mm, but a pull down diffuser enables us to use lenses down to the 18mm lens. A small cheap looking white piece of card works surprisingly well for portraits as a catch light reflector. For overall diffusion I recommend the Pro's favourite, the 'Sto-Fen' Omni-bounce. To be honest if you use on camera flash the SB26 is unlikely to be found wanting. The pre-flash system described for the built-in speedlight of the F70/N70 is enhanced to a much greater extent with the SB26 as this has a sequence of pre-flashes. In total up to 16 pre-flashes may fire before the final picture taking flash does.

The SB26 also has a beam to allow a short 1 second red-eye reduction sequence. If we set the F70/N70 to red-eye reduction and an SB26 or the built-in speedlight are not used, the red-eye reduction symbol blinks on the F70/N70 top-plate.

For those on a smaller budget the SB22 is a nice light unit with a guide number of 25m. It also has a bounce facility. Off camera flash is possible and still fully dedicated with an SC17 TTL lead, while a flash bracket, SK6 with its own connecting lead, is also available.

Q. I have an SB26. In the instruction book it refers to a feature called FP Mode flash. What is it?

A. Sadly 'not possible' is the answer. The reference to it in the speedlight's manual is a misprint.

No matter how good we become, where it is a practicality, a high quality, known brand tripod will help to improve our photography. Sharper images result and we can use longer exposure times than normal. It also allows time to study a composition comfortably from less than comfortable camera positions. If a tripod is not on your list, for whatever reason, at least think of a monopod.

Filters

One of the first accessories that many people purchase is an add on filter. The range of filters that Nikon produce is not by a long shot the world's largest, and I would be a liar if I said that I did not use filter systems comprising of a holder and drop in filters. However, I also own a sizable range of Nikon filters, probably more than most photographers, and they are optically the best - which goes some way to explain the excessive cost of them compared to the other alternatives available.

Nikon filters are produced in the following sizes - 39mm (screw fit or bayonet), 52mm, 62mm, 72mm, 77mm, 82mm, 95mm, 122mm and 160mm, all in a screw fit, as well as 2 gelatin filter holders the AF1 and AF2. There are cases for carrying a number of the smaller filters and most are supplied in sturdy plastic compartments.

Filters transmit either all of the visible spectrum but in a reduced amount, Neutral Density and Polarising, or part of the spectrum only. A filter will transmit its own colour and reduce or stop the effect of the colour opposite in the spectrum. In between, the other colours that together make up white light are affected in differing ways. In black and white work the use of a filter will change the contrast of the image by compressing or opening up the number of shades of grey recorded on the film. In colour we affect just that in the image, changing the colour completely in a subtle or dramatic way, or again changing the apparent contrast when a polarising filter is used.

Let us take a look then at the filters Nikon offer. The thread size most common is that of 52mm as the majority of lenses accept this size. All varieties of filter are produced in this size, but the larger sizes have increased in number albeit in a smaller range of options. As an example the 77mm size was first used by Nikon only in 1988 with the introduction of the 80/200mm AF f2.8 Nikkor and is available in seven different types.

The two 39mm sizes are for the very wide fisheye type lenses which, owing to the size and the curvature of the front element of the lens, accept filters at the rear of the lens as this is a smaller and more suitable area, or telephoto lenses of 300mm and 400mm with large front elements. In the case of the latter the cost of a filter for the larger front size is prohibitive and the smaller filters fit in the body or turret of the lens as the diameter of the barrel is smaller at this point. The 500mm and the 1000mm Reflex Nikkor lenses from the Manual Focus range also accept the 39mm filters. Do check to make sure that your lens takes screw in or bayonet fitments. For the telephoto lenses even longer than 400mm the 52mm size performs the same task of filtration inside the lens turret.

As an option the telephoto lenses have a gelatin filter holder for accepting non glass gels. If we want to use gels on the more conventional lenses, the AF1 with a 52mm attachment or an AF2 72mm can be used. Gelatin filters are produced in an extremely wide variety which is sometimes a restricting factor as far as camera brand filters are concerned. I use Kodak Wratten or Lee filters.

Q. I have a 62mm filter thread, can I still use gels?

A. Yes, Nikon make an adapter ring, UR1, to fit the AF2 holder on to.

The types of Nikon filter are :-

Yellow - Y44, Y48 and Y52. As with other filters that are produced in different strengths, the higher the number, the stronger the filter effect. The downside is that more light is lost due to absorption, requiring more exposure. The yellow filters are for black and white work. As yellow absorbs predominantly blue it can darken the area of a blue sky as well as cut through haze in distant shots as this is made up from the bluer end of the colour spectrum.

Orange 56 - This is again a filter for black and white work and affects the blue and green parts of the spectrum. It has the effect of darkening areas made up from these colours. I like this filter for dramatic black and white shots where the sky is predominant.

Red 60 - An incredible effect can be seen in black and white work. Shots tend to look as if they are taken at night due to a blue sky appearing nearly black. Red coloured objects, or those made up from partly red, go the other way and look lighter and this can make them look unnatural - red London buses just don't look right when shot with this filter. This is the Nikon filter recommended for certain types of infra-red work, but this is one area where the Wratten series offer more alternatives.

Green XO and X1 - Continuing the black and white arsenal, these are two filters. They absorb both red and blue. I use the X0 a lot and would recommend it as it reproduces the image in black and white closer to that seen by our eyes. The X1 is less popular but helps reproduce skin tones properly under tungsten lighting. In the field (forgive the pun) foliage is separated into individual tones better so different shades of green are reproduced as such and not condensed into a similar shade of grey.

Q. Can I use these filters with colour film?

A. Yes, but do not forget that a colour cast of the filter's colour will affect all of the image. With colour print the processing lab will often try to filter out the colour we are trying to add. It is better to let them know that a filter has been used before they print from the negatives. I personally find the whole thing a disappointment, so would suggest that colour transparency is tried as there is no filtering stage during the processing.

Neutral Density - ND2, ND4, ND8 and ND400

No effect is produced to the colour of an image. All that these filters do is reduce the light reaching the film, which happens to be more of a problem in bright light than many realise, particularly as we tend to be using slightly faster films today than a few years ago. They have also been used traditionally when duping slides and in less bright conditions when we wish to use a wide "F" stop to limit the depth of field in the image. Suitable for colour and black and white.

Polarising Filter - Don't look at the cost, look at the images is my way of summing up the polarising filter. Every journal and magazine on photography says that this should be one of the first purchases. They are right. It has also a ND effect but will saturate the colours of an image making them purer and appear stronger. The other major benefit is that reflections from windows and many other reflecting surfaces can be substantially reduced or eliminated completely in the right conditions. The only place where this will not work will be near the equator - due to the position of the sun relative to our F70 or where we have no light source at the correct angle for the light to be polarised or in sufficient strength. Nikon now only make a circular polarising filter and this allows all of the F70 features to operate. An earlier Linear filter should not be used unless we want to manually focus and use Centre-Weighted metering as it can affect both AF and Matrix metering, not detrimentally in every circumstance but it can do in many cases. Nikon make a matched lens hood especially for the polarisers which can be separated into two parts for the smaller sized filters. Together they are for longer focal lengths, but one portion can be used with shorter lenses. The HN12 is for 52mm, the HN13 for 72mm, HN26 for 62mm and HN29 for 77mm. The HN12 and HN13 can also be used on the AF1 and AF2 respectively.

Skylight - This is a filter for both mediums. As it looks predominately clear it can be left on a lens at all times as a lens protector. It reduces the blue end of the light spectrum helping to lower the effects of haze, but not as strongly as the L1BC, L37 or L39 filters.

L1BC, L37 and L39 - Are suitable for black and white or colour work. They are commonly known as haze reducing filters. The L39 absorbs more of this and is most practical for black and white work. The 26CM is multi coated to lessen the chance of internal reflections. They can again be left on all of the time.

Soft Focus Filters nos. 1 and 2 - The number 1 filter makes for pleasing portraits when attached to a lens. It helps with pictures of ladies and babies by producing a dreamy flattering effect. The number 2 is too strong for portraits, but many people do not research into its characteristics before purchase and suffer the consequences. It will be useful though for "chocolate box" type landscapes. The Soft Focus filters are far cheaper than buying a soft focus lens.

Amber Filters - Are for one of two effects. The A2 warms up an image slightly and can help with films that do not have an inherent warmth to them. The A12 converts the sensitivity of artificial light film for use in daylight.

Blue Filters - are available in three types. The B2 reduces excessive warmth when we shoot with colour in the early morning or late evening, particularly during summer months. The B8 is hardly ever used, being suited to correction of light from white flash bulbs which have a reddish tinge to them, but when was the last time you used them? Finally the B12 converts the colour from tungsten light into that suited to daylight colour film.

There are two soft cases available in which to keep the smaller filters. The CA1 will hold 6 52 or 62mm filters, while the CA2 will take 6 39mm filters.

Some other points worth clarifying are:

Linear Polarising filters should not be used as they can affect the AF system. Use circular polarisers instead. If we use strong deep coloured filters we may find that Matrix metering does not operate properly. Check with your Nikon distributor if in any doubt, or undertake your own tests to determine if a problem exists, or use Centre-Weighted or Spot metering.

Finally, use the following as a guide should you run into trouble. As the chemist might add, if symptoms persist visit your doctor or Nikon. The choice is yours. Photography is meant to be enjoyable, be patient and learn about your fine quality camera and you are half way there!

Best Wishes - John.

LCD PANEL/VIEWFINDER INDICATIONS

LCD Panel/Viewfinder	Shutter	Cause and Remedy
▭ blinks in the LCD panel.	Can be released.	Batteries are nearing exhaustion. Have a fresh one ready.
▭ blinks in the LCD panel (with or without blinking Err in the LCD panel and viewfinder).	Locked.	Batteries are just about exhausted.Turn the power off and replace battery with new one.
Err and ⊙_ blink in the LCD panel.*	Locked.	Film is not correctly positioned. Reload film.
Err DX and ISO blink in the LCD panel.*	Locked.	Non-DX-coded film or film with unacceptable DX code is loaded although auto film speed setting mode is activated. Set film speed manually.
Err and ⊙ _ blink in the LCD panel.*	Locked.	Camera back is opened during film rewind and film rewind will stop at mid-roll. To restart film rewind, press the **IN** button and **Ps** button.
⊙ blinks in the LCD panel.	Locked.	An exposed film left in the film cartridge chamber. Remove film cartridge.

* *"Err" also blinks in the viewfinder.*

LCD Panel/Viewfinder	Shutter	Cause and Remedy
blinks in the LCD panel.	Can be released.	Matrix meter is set even though lens attached has no CPU; camera automatically resets metering system to Centre-Weighted metering.
P or S blinks and F-- appears in the LCD panel.	Can be released.	Auto-Multi Program or Shutter-Priority Auto exposure mode is set even though lens attached has no CPU. Camera automatically resets exposure mode to Aperture-Priority Auto.
P_S blinks and F-- appears in the LCD panel.	Locked.	Vari-Program is set even though lens attached has no CPU.
FEE blinks in the LCD panel in Programmed Auto or Shutter-Priority Auto exposure mode.*	Locked.	Lens is not set to the smallest aperture setting. Set lens to the smallest aperture.
FEE and Programmed Auto exposure indicator (P or P_S) blink in the LCD panel* when accessory Nikon Speedlight is used.	Locked.	Attached Speedlight is not set at TTL Auto flash. Set the Speedlight flash mode to TTL, or set the camera's exposure to a mode other than Programmed Auto.

* *"Err" also blinks in the viewfinder.*

LCD Panel/Viewfinder	Shutter	Cause and Remedy
AF-S or AF-C blinks.	Locked.	Focus mode selector is set at **AF** even though a non-AF Nikkor lens is attached. Set focus mode selector to **M**.
▸ ◂ blinks in the viewfinder.	Depends on AF mode. Locked in Single Servo AF or can be released in Continuous Servo AF.	Autofocus is impossible with the subject. Set focus mode selector to **M** and focus manually using clear matte field.
◂ stays in the viewfinder in AF mode.	Depends on AF mode. Locked in Single Servo AF or can be released in Continuous Servo AF.	Subject is located closer than the closest focusing distance of the lens. Move away from subject and refocus.
Hi blinks in Auto exposure mode.	Can be released.	Overexposure possible.
Lo blinks in Auto exposure mode.	Can be released.	Underexposure possible.

LCD Panel/Viewfinder	Shutter	Cause and Remedy
bulb blinks.	Locked.	a) "Bulb" is set in the Shutter-Priority Auto exposure mode. Set exposure mode to Manual or set another shutter speed. b) You set All Mode Exposure Bracketing with a shutter speed set at "Bulb". To use All Mode Exposure Bracketing, select another shutter speed setting.
Shutter speed indication blinks inside viewfinder in Programmed Auto or Aperture-Priority Auto Exposure mode.	Can be released.	Automatically selected shutter speed is 1/50 sec. or slower and picture blur may occur due to camera shake. To reduce possibility of blur, hold camera very steady, use a tripod or use the built-in flash or an accessory Nikon Speedlight. Selecting a wider aperture (smaller f-number) results in a faster shutter speed.
Shutter speed indication in the LCD panel and viewfinder blinks.	Can be released.	You are performing All Mode Exposure Bracketing in Manual exposure mode.

LCD Panel/Viewfinder	Shutter	Cause and Remedy
Shutter speed indication in the LCD panel blinks and 125 is indicated inside viewfinder in flash photography.	Can be released.	You set shutter speed faster than 1/125 sec. and shutter speed automatically shifts to 1/125 sec.
H or L blinks in the LCD panel.	Can be released.	Built-in flash or accessory Nikon Speedlight is turned on with film advance mode set for continuous shooting. Camera automatically resets film advance mode to single-frame shooting (S).
[ ] blinks in LCD panel and [•] appears inside the viewfinder.	Can be released.	Built-in flash or accessory Nikon Speedlight is turned on with Wide Area focus. Camera automatically resets focus area to Spot.
Green ⚡ lights up inside the viewfinder.	Can be released.	Your subject is too dark. Use built-in flash or Nikon Speedlight.
Red ⚡ blinks inside the viewfinder after flash shooting.	Can be released.	Light might have been insufficient. Confirm shooting distance and, if necessary, move closer to the subject or select a wider aperture.

LCD Panel/Viewfinder	Shutter	Cause and Remedy
blinks in the LCD panel.	Can be released.	Red-Eye Reduction is set with Speedlight other than the Nikon SB-26. Camera automatically switches flash sync mode to Normal Sync.

ABOUT LCD

- The F70/F70D uses a Liquid Crystal Display (LCD) of the highest quality which, under conditions of normal use, should provide several years of reliable operation. After this period contrast may deteriorate and display information may start to fade. You can have the LCD replaced at a nominal charge by contacting an authorised Nikon dealer or service facility.
- At high temperatures of 60°C or above, the display turns black, making it impossible to read. It returns to normal when the temperature drops to 20°C.
- At temperatures below freezing, the LCD's response time slows down; it goes back to normal when the temperature rises.

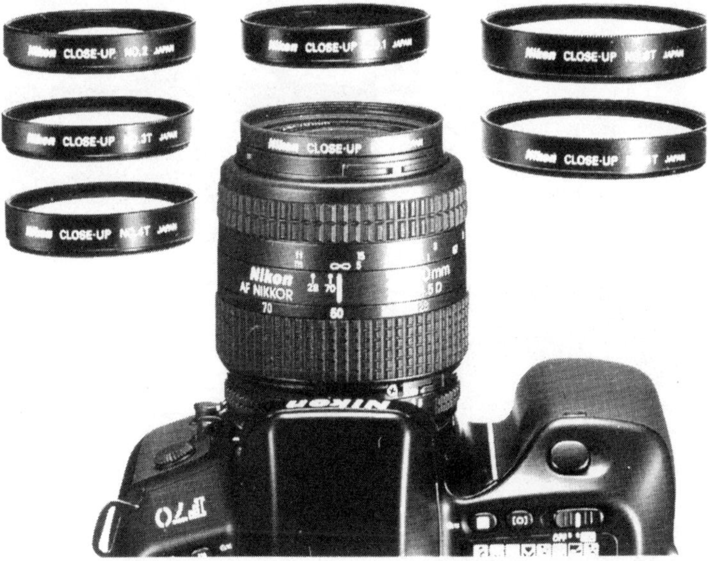

Nikon close-up accessories
You get close focusing with every AF Zoom-Nikkor lens, but you can get even closer with an AF Micro-Nikkor— the ultimate in close-up sharpness and overall focusing range. You can also choose a close-up attachment, available in 0, 1, 2, 3T, 4T, 5T and 6T versions.

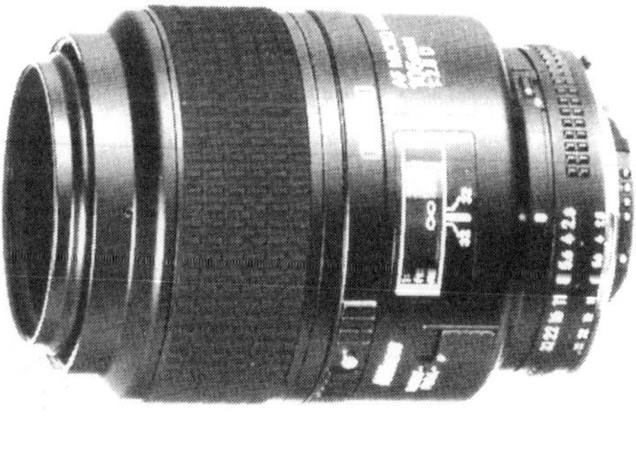

ACCESSORIES WELL WORTH LOOKING AT!

OP/TECH

The world's most comfortable cameras, bag and tripod straps (binoculars too). Op/tech has a built-in weight reduction system that makes equipment feel 50% lighter and 100% more comfortable. From the famous 'Pro-Camera Strap' to the 'Bag Strap' and the 'Tripod Strap', the style, colours and comfort which along with the non-slip grip, ensure that you have a wonderful combination of comfort and safety.

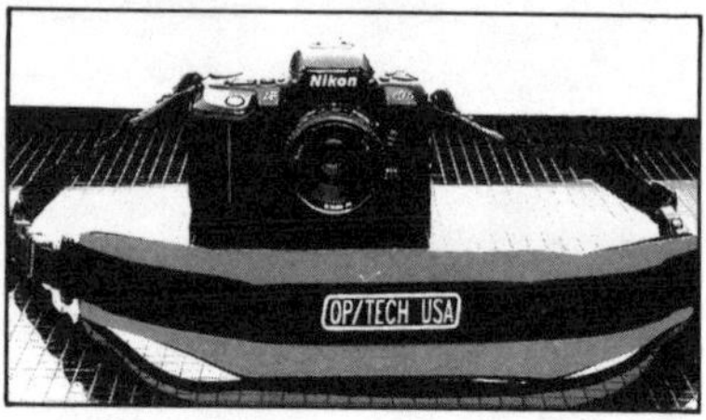

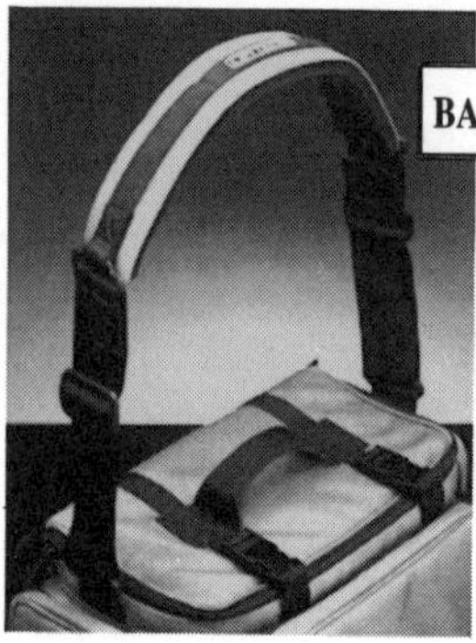

BAG STRAP

The **OP/TECH USA Bag Strap** is the answer to the problem of carrying a heavy bag for extended periods of time. By combining the patented weight reduction system with the Non Slip Grip™, you have the perfect strap for camera/video bags and cases as well as garment bags. Adjustable from 29" to 52", this strap is one of a kind. You will feel the difference!

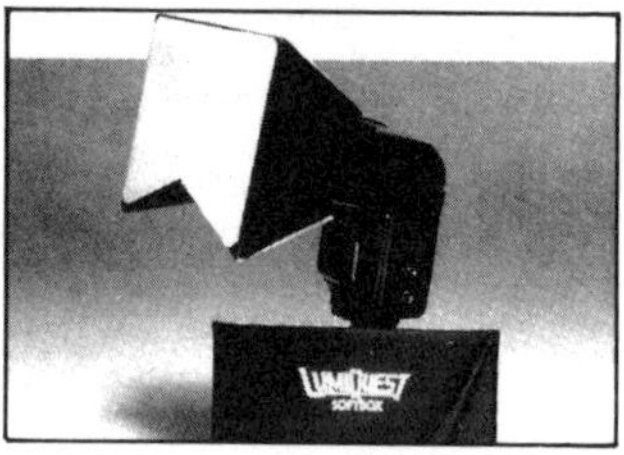

LUMIQUEST

For any portable flashgun that has a bounce head. Lumiquest is an accessory system that has a place in everybody's camera bag. Not just to reduce 'red-eye', but from the simple 'Pocket Bounce' through to the 'Softbox', added diffusion for flash portrait or close-up's of still life can be achieved while at the same time Metallic Inserts in silver will give spectacular highlights and in gold, a warm sunset tone. Snoots and Barndoors are part of the system for the creative flash photographer.

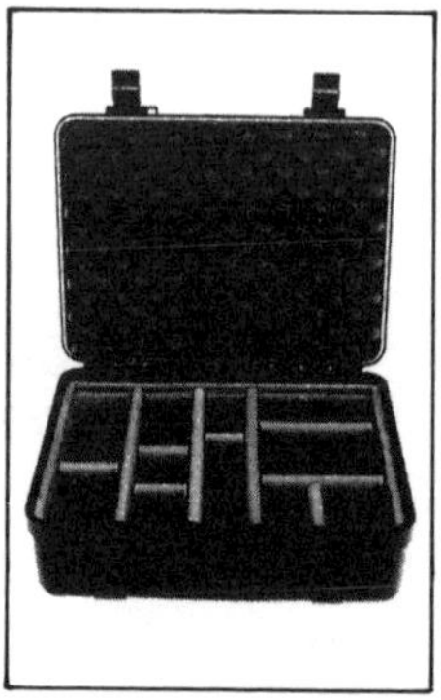

PELI-PELICAN CASES

Watertight and airtight to 30 feet for the ultimate in protection. Constructed of light weight space age structural resin with a neoprene "O" ring seal and exclusive purge valve. Supplied complete with pre-scored pick n'pluck foam or padded dividers. Also includes locking flanges, massive multiple latches for absolute security and best of all, a comfortable molded grip handle.

Also Available from Hove Foto Books

HOVE FOTO BOOKS

Hove Foto Books is the premier English language publisher of camera user's guides and books on Modern Collectors Cameras. The following is a brief listing of other books of interest available from Hove Foto Books.

Hove Camera and Accessory Manuals

"Super How-To Books..." The Washington Post

These complete user's guides are "take-along" manuals, small enought to fit in a camera bag. Hove camera manuals explain the correct operation of the equipment in much greater detail than the camera's instruction book. They include general picture-taking advice and are thoroughly illustrated. Approximately 176 pages. Paperbound with stay-clean, laminated covers.

Available for the world's most popular "SLR" cameras, and the following Nikon equipment:

Nikon F4/F4S/F4E/F3
Nikon F401s, F-401/N5005, N4004
Nikon F-801s/N8008s
Nikon F601, F-601M/N6006, N6000
Nikon F-90/N-90
Nikon SB-25 Flash
Nikon SB-24 Flash
Nikon F50/N50
Nikon F70/N70

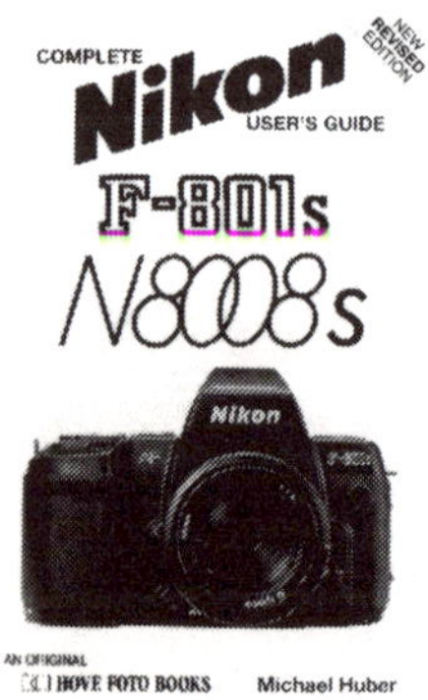

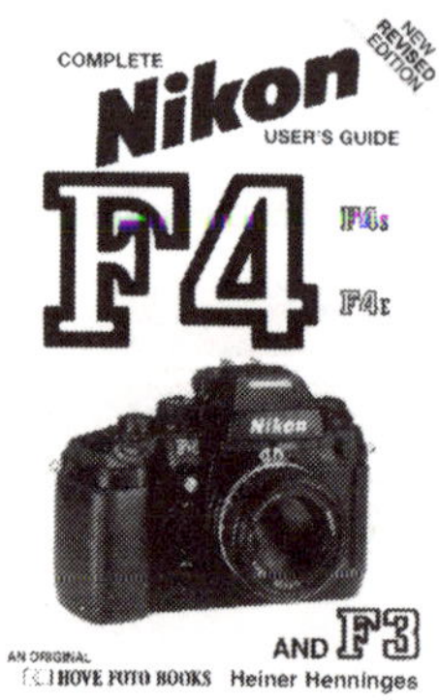